INVITING A MONKEY TO TEA

DISCOVER LASTING CONTENTMENT

NANCY COLIER

MJF BOOKS
NEW YORK

Published by MJF Books
Fine Communications
322 Eighth Avenue
New York, NY 10001

Inviting a Monkey to Tea
LC Control Number: 2014937494
ISBN 978-1-60671-253-5

Interior design and layout by Becky Fulker, Kubera Book Design, Prescott, Arizona

The poem "The Guest House" by Rumi, translated by Coleman Barks from
The Illuminated Rumi [Broadway Books, 1997], used with the gracious permission
of the translator.

This edition is published by MJF Books in arrangement with Hohm Press.

Author's Disclaimer:
To maintain privacy, all the names in this book have been changed. In addition,
for the purposes of explanation, some of the individuals used in the examples
are composites of several different people. Lastly, as I do not use recording devices,
the quotes are from memory and in some cases, are re-created to demonstrate
the process that transpires.

Printed in the United States of America.

MJF Books and the MJF colophon are trademarks of Fine Creative Media, Inc.

QF   10 9 8 7 6 5 4 3 2 1

For Juliet, Frederic, and Gretchen

ACKNOWLEDGEMENTS

Most of all, I am profoundly grateful to my family for their support and love throughout the creation of this book.

To my daughter, Juliet, you have been so proud of me during this writing process, as I have been of you. You have patiently and cheerfully put up with me being squirreled away in my office, made me laugh every single day, always taken my side (as I will always take yours), and howled bad words into the wind with me. You bring the joy and sweetness to my life, which makes the hard work possible. You are my most profound delight—my heart—and the love that reminds me of who I am. You are the stuff that this book is all about.

To my husband Frederic, you have relentlessly encouraged me, reminded me that I am the one with content, pushed me to trust my own wisdom, advised me on when to step away, and held my hand when I cried. When everyone was diving in the pool, you found me a chair in the shade so that I could work. Thank you for rubbing my feet, taking Alice out when I am tired, and saving my technological life—over and over again—with patience and skill, and never a drop of irritation. Thank you too, for your willingness—to take this adventure of life, and for your unceasing loyalty. You are my dearest friend.

And to my daughter, Gretchen, who was baking while I wrote this book, thank you for the great journey that your creation has been, and for poking your nose up through that inner tube in the vast ocean. You are my true gift.

I am so grateful to my mother, Diane Shainberg. You gave me the experience of being loved, unconditionally, an experience that I carry forever. You always saved the seat next to you, for me. Thank you for steeping me in your sense of wonder and reverence for life, and for knowing that there is so much more. So too, I am grateful to you for marinating me in the teachings of those who are now my teachers. I am also deeply grateful to my friend, Jan Bronson, for your presence, support, understanding, guidance and comfort over so many years. From un-tethered to free, we have traveled together. You have been profoundly important in my life. While you claim to hold only four options in any situation, in truth, you have helped me create a life of infinite possibilities. I am grateful to Loch Kelly, who has been a tremendous source of inspiration and guidance. You were the first person to put precise words to what I was experiencing in my practice. You continually offer me tools that inform and enrich my evolution. And to Catherine Ingram, your no-nonsense wisdom, sense of humor, and grounded advice has offered me a clear vision for how this path can be lived. You are a true role model. To Gangaji, your fierce grace and infinite kindness has been priceless in my journey. I feel your support. And to Mooji, I am so grateful to have found you. You remind, point and usher me into what I really am. Thank you to Betsy Robinson, my first editor. We were supposed to meet. I am so grateful that the universe did its part in making that happen. Your enthusiasm and deep understanding of the material refueled my process.

A big thank you to Regina Sara Ryan, my editor at Hohm Press. You have been a remarkable source of insight, warmth and encouragement. You were the first person to actually be able to help me with the contents of my material. To have a woman of your spiritual weight and substance going to bat for me, has been deeply nourishing and invigorating. Your belief in my work changed me. And to Rick Lewis, who helped me remember who I am in this process, and what I can and want to offer. Your capacity to listen and understand inspired my process.

Acknowledgements

And to my dear friend, Laurie Niehoff, with whom I can play in the highest of realms, and the silliest. You have generously offered your expansive intelligence and kindness throughout the creation of this book. I respect your judgment and trust you, always.

Thank you to my agent, Laura Yorke, for believing in this project. Your energy and experience revitalized the proposal process and gave the book the boost it needed.

And finally, I am deeply grateful to my clients, for the time we get to spend together, and for your willingness and courage to seek the truth. You give me the chance to fall in and into love every day.

Thank you to all of you.

CONTENTS

INTRODUCTION

Stop for a moment, before you read any further. Stop and notice what you are thinking, and how many thoughts are passing in and out of your awareness right now. Probably too many to count, with one thought coming directly after another, overlapping, with little thread connecting one to the next. If this is the case you are a normal human being. In Buddhism, it is said that the human mind is like a monkey in a cage who has drunk a bottle of wine and been stung by a bee. The monkey is wild and usually frantic. We all have one of these monkeys living inside us, yammering on about this or that, screeching its opinions and ideas, without stopping to take a breath.

Our monkeys come with their own quirks and preferences, memories, feelings, stories and ways of processing information. They babble on with or without our permission, ceaselessly. The problem is not that we house a monkey, but that we believe that we *are* that monkey, that we defer our identity to the monkey and follow behind these mad creatures as if they were in a position to guide us. In truth, we are much larger than the monkey that lives inside us.

In order to enjoy *who we really are*, we must move beyond the monkey mind, to that which sits below it, in and around the thoughts and feelings. We must discover the *I* that can hear the monkey but is not merged with it. In many spiritual traditions, they speak of taking no interest in the mind's output, paying the mind no mind if you will. And yet, after many years of working with the mind, I have found that we cannot go directly from being identified with our mind to simply disregarding it. Unfortunately, we still believe most of what our mind tells us; we think its thoughts are true, and are aligned with the feelings that result from thoughts. Consequently, to disregard our mind is not a workable plan. And yet, when we find it impossible to pay no mind to the mind, we demand something else impossible, namely, that the mind become something it isn't: calm, quiet and well behaved. This is not a viable option either—insisting that the monkey become a house cat. It is not about the mind becoming different, but rather about our realizing that we are not it, and thus realizing *who we really are.*

Before we can move beyond mind, we must first develop a caring and inclusive relationship with it. We cannot just dump it on the side of the road and expect things to go well. We need to care about the monkey that is trapped inside us, the wild animal who believes its fears, believes that it must do, strive and make everything happen, and most of all, that there is nothing else beyond "it." We must bring a loving kindness to its fears of extinction, its drive to survive, not knowing anything other than what it knows. We, the larger awareness, need to offer the mind a seat at our inner table so that it does not feel abandoned, and thus, even more desperate.

In the process of welcoming our mind, allowing it to be what it is, we learn that we do not need to agree with it, fear it, or even have it calm down. We learn to go about our life and know ourselves with the monkey simply spouting off in the background. When we invite our monkey to tea, it is with a friendly and open heart; we are not angry at our monkey for being a monkey and not demanding that it be different than what it is by nature. The monkey can go on being a monkey and we can appreciate it for its monkey-ness— from where *we are*, which is everywhere. It is not that the mind is tamed by way of offering it tea, but rather that we are separate from it and re-identified with that presence as the larger awareness, which is big enough to house even this wild creature called mind.

As you move through this book, I encourage you to practice inviting your own monkey to tea—paying attention to your own thoughts as they arise while you are reading and after. Slowly, you may notice that *who you are* is changing—from being the monkey, to empathizing with the monkey, to simply letting the monkey *monkey around* inside you—without having to pay it much mind. Enjoy the tea party!

BEYOND HAPPINESS

The drive to be happy, I believe, is innate in the human species. We all want to be happy. What is not innate in the human species however, and yet remarkably prevalent in monkey minds of all kinds, are the following two thoughts. One: we are supposed to be (and stay) happy. Two: we must *do* something to create that happiness. For the most part, we believe these thoughts. Everyone, everywhere, is trying to find, create, invent—and hold onto—happiness. We do everything we are supposed to do: diligently follow the instructions, practice the techniques, and still, more often than we should be (given the amount of effort we are putting in), we are not happy. As a psychotherapist and interfaith minister, I have spent the last two decades witnessing people and myself feed their addiction to happiness; we get our short term fix here and there, but end up *back on the street* searching for happiness yet again, even more desperate. I have watched as those who are put off by the happiness market and uncomfortable with or intimidated by the spiritual path, end up lost at sea, not knowing where to turn to feel better. In truth, we are all lost at sea when it comes to happiness. The thing we want most and spend the majority of our time trying to accomplish eludes us.

I am an optimist. I believe that we human beings are remarkable creatures, that we can do anything we set out to do. So why not happiness? Why is there such a split between our desire for happiness and our ability to find it? After many years of listening to people talk about their failed attempts to hang onto a state of happiness, I began asking myself the following questions: What is this thing we call happiness? Is it achievable? Is it reliable? Is it sustainable? If it is, why are we *not* happy so much of the time?

As I studied the state of happiness, I became intensely aware of its fragility. When our life circumstances change and we lose the object that's been making us happy... poof, our happiness is gone. When uncomfortable feelings appear within our state of happiness, our grip on happiness is lost. When the object that was bringing us happiness no longer *delivers* the same effect, we are lost again. We are constantly acquiring and losing happiness.

Happiness relies on controlling circumstances that, no matter how hard we try, we cannot control. It relies on circumstances staying the same. Life's circumstances do not—ever—stay the same. This is the nature of life. And yet, it is not our efforts to create happiness that are flawed; we are not doing anything wrong. But rather than chasing happiness, steadfastly defending the belief that somewhere, somehow, if we find the right thing, we will indeed be able to hold onto happiness for good, we need to find a new goal, one that is related to *this* life. Quite simply, happiness is the wrong goal for *this* life.

And yet, despite the fact that happiness is consistently inconsistent, permanently impermanent, we judge ourselves as failures when we cannot maintain a perpetual state of happiness. People who are not happy are viewed as failures; it is our fault that we cannot hold onto a permanent state of happiness. We are not trying hard enough, not living our life right. Regardless of unceasing evidence to the contrary, we continue to demand and expect that happiness be something it isn't—that life be something that it isn't.

For me personally, happiness arrived as a two-sided coin; on one side was the object of my happiness and on the other, my fear of losing it. With happiness so married to loss, I was chronically reminded of the impending doom that accompanied happiness. My fear and sadness about this truth then whittled away at any enjoyment of the happiness attained.

This is a book for everyone who has ever tried to create a lasting state of happiness—and failed. So too, it is a book for everyone who is uninspired or put off by the happiness market, but who still wants to feel better than they feel.

And so the question begs—is there something larger, deeper, more lasting than happiness? Is there a state of *being*—a state of well-*being*, within which contentment arises and endures, sustained in the midst of the changing circumstances and emotional shifts that life includes?

Is there a way to feel grounded and well even when the contents of our life are not that way? If so, what skill or quality must we have, what action must we take, what shift must we make to create this state of well-*being* that is deeper and larger than happiness?

As a student of Advaita Vedanta and Buddhism, I have been practicing awareness and meditation for a long time. For a good part of that time, I was using my spiritual practice to try to make me a feel a different way than the way I felt, or maybe more accurately, to take me somewhere else internally—anywhere other than where I was. Peace and happiness were the goal for my spiritual practice. And indeed this was a goal that I accomplished, in stretches. And yet, again and again, when life presented its toughest challenges, inevitably and consistently, the peace and happiness that I had achieved on the meditation cushion slipped away.

Somewhere along the path I got tired—luckily. I got tired of trying to get to peace and happiness, or rather, of getting there and then watching it disintegrate. And with my weariness came an interesting development. Rather than taking my seat on the cushion to find peace and happiness, I took my seat to *uncover what was true*, my actual state. At some point, I decided to stop trying to do anything with or to what was happening inside me, to demand that it become something else, and I just let myself experience what I was experiencing.

I suppose you could say that I stopped using my meditation practice as an object whose purpose was to provide me with something, transport me somewhere else, make *me* someone else. My meditation practice could then be what it was, my mind could be what it was, whatever that meant on any particular day. It was through this shift that I began to glimpse a state of being that is steadfastly okay, even when our circumstances are not okay—a state that is deeper and more eternal than happiness. A peaceful, contented state that fed on what was real, here, and now. Indeed, it was not until I stopped relating to happiness as an object to be gained, stopped searching for happiness—as a way out—and started searching for *what is*—as a way in—that I discovered a doorway to somewhere far more blissful than happiness had ever taken me.

THE PROMISE OF THIS BOOK

Normal life is not easy for anyone. As someone who speaks to people all day and also lives in this world, I can say that with one-hundred-percent certainty. Why then do we expect ourselves to be happy all the time? This foolish expectation creates tremendous and unnecessary suffering. Rather than trying to hang onto something whose nature it is to come and go, we need to shift our attention to creating a state of being that can withstand the volatility of a real life—relationships, work, health, finances—all of it. This book is not another self-help gimmick, another expert telling you that you can be happy all the time and if you are not it is your fault. Such statements are false. Happiness is wonderful, I am all for it, the more the better. We should be grateful for happiness when it is here, but as a goal for our life, it is unwise.

We spend our lives trying to get to some imaginary *there*, where happiness awaits. What we don't know how to do is to get to *here*, where we are and where well-being and contentment lives. Well-being is an internal state, not dependent upon external circumstances. It is a result of our attitude toward our feelings, not the nature of the feelings themselves and not the circumstances that are causing the feelings. It is the comfort we offer ourselves when disappointment is the cloud in our sky, the gratitude that we invoke when joy floats through, the kindness that we offer whatever feelings pass into and out of our inner landscape, regardless of what they may be.

So too, well-being is an ongoing process and not an object that we obtain (after which time it will be safe to go back to sleep in our life). True well-being can only happen when we are paying attention to the now; it devolves into an intellectual concept when *applied* to the past or future. The substance of well-being is our own compassionate presence—the compassion and presence that we bring to our own experience.

We discover well-being when we shift the direction of our glance toward this moment and what is actually here. The secret to well-being is oddly counter-intuitive: allow whatever is happening inside you to happen. That's it. Don't *do* anything with it. Simply notice the sensations that you are feeling, hear the thoughts that you are thinking—allow all of it to happen—without trying to change or judge it, and—without identifying with its contents. Invite your monkey mind to tea, with all its wildness, as you would a friend who has many interesting and not so interesting stories to tell. When you let go of controlling your mind's output, accomplishing something with it, and simply meet your mind, as it is, with a sense of delight and compassion, appreciation for its particularities, you will find the *you* who is in fact hearing the thoughts, feeling the sensations, experiencing your experience—the *you* who is not the monkey mind—the *you* who is always well.

In truth, we have been chasing raindrops oblivious to the fact that we are already swimming in an ocean of contentment. Contentment is here, awaiting our presence. It is we who turn away from it, believing that the raindrops are our best hope. This book is about learning to shift the direction of our journey, from *out and away from* to *into and toward* ourselves, into what is actually happening here, now, our true nature. Contentment can only flourish within our own presence in what is, and only once we realize that we are not the monkey mind. Throughout these pages, I invite you into a state of being and a state of *you* that is deeper than happiness, one that can support us and keep us eternally okay.

I offer this book as a road map of sorts, from chasing happiness to discovering well-being and lasting contentment. My hope is that the experience of reading the book will serve as a microcosm of the larger change process I describe, that is—from believing that you must heed whatever your mind tells you, to compassionately caring for your mind even if you don't believe it. So too, my wish is that your sense of who you actually *are* will shift and open as the pages turn, and that you will come to know yourself, not just as the mind's contents, but as the infinite and loving awareness within which the monkey creates its mischief. And away we go…

THE GUEST HOUSE

This being human is a guest house.
Every morning a new arrival.

A joy, a depression, a meanness,
some momentary awareness comes
as an unexpected visitor.

Welcome and entertain them all!
Even if they are a crowd of sorrows,
who violently sweep your house
empty of its furniture,
still, treat each guest honorably.
He may be clearing you out
for some new delight.

The dark thought, the shame, the malice.
meet them at the door laughing and invite them in.

Be grateful for whatever comes.
because each has been sent
as a guide from beyond.

> —Jelaluddin Rumi, translation by Coleman Barks.
> Used with permission.

PART ONE:

HAPPINESS VS. WELL-BEING

1 ADDICTED TO HAPPINESS

Happiness is an addiction and we are *hooked*. Happiness is an addiction because our monkey mind convinces us that we are not okay if we don't get our fix of it. It is an addiction because it provides relief for short periods of time and then fails us over and over again. It is an addiction because we are consumed with the need to be happy. We spend an enormous amount of time and energy trying to make happiness happen, and yet we remain not happy.

There is a belief in this culture that life is supposed to be happy; happiness is part of our definition of a good life. In the face of the suffering that everyone's life contains, we hold tight to our belief that life's basic nature is pleasurable and fun. The media presents life as some kind of amusement park ride with ice cream, laughter and prizes. Our conception of what we are supposed to feel is based on a life that is not in alignment with what's real. Certainly, a part of life is joy. Life is also challenging and difficult at times. All of these experiences are part of the ride. We have to do things that we don't want to do, we have to interact with people who hurt us, we have to live inside a body that gets sick, and eventually we have to let go of everyone that we love. Expecting a joy ride is a recipe for disappointment. And yet the cultural mythology persists: life is *supposed* to look good, smell good, and be fun all the time.

In this society, when we are not happy, not only are we failures for not being able to create a happy life, but worse, we are missing out on the myth. We are not getting what we deserve—what everyone else undoubtedly gets. With such a cultural mythology, we spend much of our life feeling depressed about not getting to have something that doesn't exist, thereby fueling the un-happiness that we so dread.

I was one who suffered with this belief system in my younger years. A friend and fellow sufferer called it her "Kennedy life." We are convinced that for other people, life is one long series of touch football games held on large glorious lawns with large glorious extended families, and golden retrievers joyously chasing blond toddlers in playful tackle. When we are reminded that the Kennedy family has also endured tragedy—violence and loss—we take the information in, but only on an intellectual level. We know that the Kennedys have suffered; we know that they have grown through suffering and devoted their lives to service, but still our touch football expectation of life endures. In fact, we struggle to retain this fantasy. It makes us un-happy, but at the same time, we are afraid to stop trying to get happy.

We make strong judgments about the person who achieves happiness, and the one who doesn't. Happiness is our flag of success. Not being able to accomplish it means that there is something wrong with us. As a family member recently confessed, "If I am not happy then I am just a big loser."

As a result of these beliefs, we are left in a desperate state. We must be vigilant in controlling our experience, making sure that it feels good, making sure that we are succeeding at this happiness game. But making the present moment feel good is a lot of work. Happiness is a narrow destination at which to aim our life with an even narrower selection of paths for getting there—a bit like fixating on a bird in flight and never seeing the sky. We have balanced our okay-ness on something as ephemeral and uncontrollable as situational pleasure, and bet our well-being on our ability to keep ourselves here—with no net below if we fall or fail. We dedicate the majority of our energy to achieving something that we cannot consistently achieve. From a purely logical perspective, it seems that it would be wise to re-examine our goal.

COMFORTABLE WITH UN-HAPPINESS

Our attempts to be happy are not the problem. The problem is that we are not aware of a workable alternative to happiness. As we see it, the only alternative to happiness is sadness, which is an uninhabitable condition. We do not know how to live with un-happiness, a state that is neither happy nor sad. We do not know how to be without happiness and still be okay, or even that it is possible—at least not yet.

Jenna looked shocked when I first mentioned the idea of *not* being happy with the circumstances of her life *and* still being okay. "Why on earth would I want to get okay with less than happiness?" she asked, nearly bolting from my office. It was clear that I was not the therapist for her if my plan was to help her become comfortable with less happiness. "So you want me to surrender to misery? Is that the purpose of therapy?" Obviously, this is not what I meant by getting okay with un-happiness. I rephrased, explaining that we needed to find a way to be okay even when the contents of our lives were not pleasing. As I said to Jenna, "Finding a way to be okay is not the same thing as surrendering to misery."

Happiness in this culture means that we like our life situation. Our experience of the present moment is positive; the contents of our lives are pleasing. From my friend Rob: "Happy? I guess that means I feel good, things are going well. Not a very complicated way of putting it, but ultimately, I am having a good time in my life." Or as my daughters' babysitter described, "I am feeling pleasure, that's happiness for me." As definitions of happiness go, having a good time or feeling pleasure is as good as any other.

Un-happy is not a place that we know how to inhabit. It is not a place where we know how to console ourselves. It is not a place where we can be peaceful or feel good about ourselves. It is not a place that includes company or a place we can move through or learn from. It is not a place that we want to be, under any conditions.

We are given no training in how to ease our discomfort and soothe our sadness, as if these states were not a part of a regular life, a good life. We are instructed to keep our chin up, make lemons out of lemonade, get on with it. Or put another way; get *away* from it—whatever is making us un-happy. We have never been taught how to take care of ourselves and our un-happiness in a way that can still leave us feeling well.

We are trained to believe that un-happiness is a scary thing, not only because we do not know how to manage it, but also because it makes us unlovable. We are scary to others when we are un-happy; it is not just that we are afraid of ourselves, but others are afraid of us as well. Un-happiness leaves us helpless and abandoned, and therefore it must be avoided at all costs.

"I stay in the house when I'm not happy," said Debbie. "People don't want to be around you when you're not happy. It's like you're like a leper. If you get too close, they might catch what you have. But the truth is, I also don't want to expose my friends to my misery. Why should they have to sit through my mess? And what fun would I be anyway if I'm bummed out? Nobody wants a Debbie Downer around. When I can see the glass as half full again, I will be someone to hang out with." Un-happiness is viewed as a cultural disease, and one we consider contagious.

When Debbie experienced un-happiness, she feared that her friends would shun her and find her repelling. "Eew . . . it's sort of repulsive. I know my friends want to be around someone happy, upbeat, not some whole dark trip." Our associations with un-happiness are filled with rejection and repulsion. Paula decided to ride out her sadness alone in her apartment with a pint of ice cream as company and comfort. "I'll be out again when I am presentable," she said, not realizing the tragedy of her words.

We have designed a system that demands that we stay happy; it is a system that relies upon our control over something that ultimately cannot be controlled. And the alternative, un-happiness, is dreadful, frightening, and riddled with self-loathing. Despite the consistently transient, challenging, and uncontrollable nature of life, we continue to insist that life can be and indeed *is* ceaselessly pleasing; we continue to demand and expect happiness.

SELF-HELP AND THE SEARCH FOR HAPPINESS

In order to serve our constant need for happiness—to be having a good time—we have created a billion dollar self-help industry bloated with psychological and spiritual gurus, all teaching us how to ceaselessly enjoy the contents of our life. This is not to say that real gurus do not exist. They do and the right master at the right time can change our life. Nonetheless, the stream of self-help experts and self-improvement programs that fills and refills our bookstore shelves is unending. Faster than we can even digest the back covers of their happily packaged products, the self-help industry generates and markets a new crop of shiny covers, bright-eyed faces, and solutions to life's *life-ness*. But despite the gigantic quantity, modern self-help generally falls into one of just three camps.

The first self-help camp (positive thinking, the law of attraction, manifesting your life, etc.) sells us programs on how to take control of our life situation—to create a life situation that is to our liking and pleasurable. The first camp tells us that we will receive whatever we put out into the world; it is all up to us.

The second camp (cognitive-behavioral therapy, mind control, etc.) teaches us how to control our feelings *about* the contents of our life. This camp teaches us how to make sure that, at the end of the day, our feelings about our life situation fall into the plus column. Once again, it is up to us to control how we feel about our life—and it should be good!

The third camp takes a different approach; it instructs us on how to bypass our human experience altogether and proceed directly to a transcendent state, where what happens personally to us does not really matter. Like other camps, this form of misguided spirituality supports our belief that we cannot experience un-happiness and also be okay, even well.

Imagine a three-tiered system. The first tier is the situation of our life, what is going on for us. The second tier is our experience of that life situation, the way we feel *about* what is happening. The third tier is how we relate to, behave toward, and in general, what we do with our feelings about our life situation. We not only have an emotional response to every situation, we also have a response to our response. Say we have a fight with a friend. The fight is the situation, the first tier. Next we have our feelings about the fight, our experience of what happened. In this case, the second tier might contain anger and rejection. And finally, the third tier is made up of everything that we say and do to our anger and rejection—the relationship that we build with our own feelings. While our search for happiness transpires in the first two tiers, well-being is created in the third tier, in the relationship we conduct with ourselves and our experience. But before I travel any further down the path of well-being, I will outline the systems designed to keep us happy in more detail, and why they fail.

The "Make It Happen" School of Happiness

The make-it-happen school of happiness is focused almost entirely on taking control of our life situation. We must figure out a way to control things so that we never need to experience difficult emotions. The system relies on the theory that our internal world will follow our external world. If we make our external world pleasurable, our internal experience will be pleasurable as well. The leaders of this school prescribe vision boarding, affirmations, and other techniques to manifest our desires and bring us a pleasurable life. Create the life you want and you will be happy; it makes sense. The problem is that it does not work on a consistent basis, or for that matter on a practical level—not with life as it is.

The system fails when things don't go the way we visualized, collaged, and mindfully intended. The closest I've seen to an

...ining this situation—not getting the job—from a third ...pective, what kind of relationship did we build with our ...on? What did we do with the feelings that were there? ...ely, we rejected them. We told ourselves that our frustra-...r actual experience, was wrong and unacceptable. The rela-...we built with our experience was one of judgment, repu-..., and abandonment. As a result, we were forced into a kind ...tional box, a way we were supposed to feel despite what was ...urthermore, the box was to serve as our key to happiness, as if ...ness could ever come from something other than what is true ...ore on that later).

"Witness Protection" School of Happiness

...help traps lay in the spiritual world as well, well-intentioned ...s that lead us astray—away from both happiness and well-be-...Many spiritual schools teach us to become observers of our ...minds, our own reactions, and our own experience. This is a ...foundly helpful and liberating skill. Becoming aware of our own ...d is the beginning of true well-being and something we will ...much more about in coming chapters. Yet, even within these ...ools of spirituality, we are sometimes led off course. While spiri-...al approaches are less inclined to encourage us to control our life ...uation or manage our experience in order to achieve happiness, ...irituality—like self-help—can be used as a way to bypass or avoid ...ur own experience.

In becoming a witness to our experience, we can become indif-...erent to it, dismissive even, with the idea that rising above the con-...ditions of our life or how we feel about those conditions is somehow ...spiritual maturity and will lead to well-being. As I was busy strug-...gling with *not trying hard enough* in my spiritual practice, a fellow ...spiritual traveler and friend appeared to be falling into the bypass ...trap. "This is great," he told me after a difficult argument with his ...wife, "whatever happens, whatever I feel, it doesn't really matter. I

explanation of what to do when we're *left out in the cold* is the instruction, *try harder*. Ultimately, however, if we are not able to make our dreams come true, there is nothing to support us further on our path to happiness. We are sent on our way as failures.

Jane, a dear friend and fellow type A compatriot, was unhappily single. Always up for a new strategy for improving her life, she enrolled in the make-it-happen school of happiness and committed to taking control of her situation. The plan: she would take responsibility for attracting the perfect man into her life. A good student, she hung clippings of her ideal mate in each room of her apartment, cleared out half her closet in preparation for his crisp oxford shirts, placed two roses in each of her window vases, and completed the daily affirmations, visualizations, and mantras that invited him into her heart and life. But after months of doing all the right things, still, her dance card remained empty.

Jane felt defeated, disappointed and ashamed about her inability to create a relationship and manifest her desires. What then was Jane going to do with her feelings of disappointment and shame? What kind of relationship was she going to build with her experience? She could take the side of her own experience, comfort her disappointment, and reassure her shame, or she could turn against it, judge it, blame it, or otherwise reject it. The critical choice for Jane awaited here in this third tier, and it would be the real test of how she would live this challenging life situation. Her choice of how to relate to her own feelings would determine whether well-being would be given the opportunity to emerge in her life, and whether she could free herself from the wheel of suffering that is happiness or un-happiness. Unfortunately, in this case, the make-it-happen school of happiness escorted Jane down the path to suffering.

Jane consulted her new guru whose advice regarding her still-single status (as well as her frustration and sadness) was to manifest more diligently than she had already manifested. Basically, try harder, do more. (Dangerous advice for us type A's!) Perhaps she had allowed negative thoughts to enter her energy field or had not visualized her future husband with enough clarity. Either way, the implication was that Jane had created or at least failed to un-create the negative situation that she was now in. Having created the situation, she was also responsible for creating the painful feelings that she was experiencing. In short, she was to blame for her own suffering. Consequently, Jane's relationship with her own experience was filled with anger and criticism. She was angry at her own disappointment, and disappointed by her own shame. Jane's feelings served as reminders of her failure and inadequacy. Unconsciously, she told her experience that *it* (and thus she) was un-deserving of care, comfort, or even a listening ear, given that she had no one to blame but herself.

Jane is an example of how and where this approach to happiness fails. When our life situation is challenging and we are unable to make the external situation change, we need to be on our side, to be kind to ourselves, and to take good care of the experience we are having as a result of the situation at hand. But more often than not, this is where the system breaks down and where the real suffering begins. On graduation day, Jane went home without a partner, but accompanied by a newly strengthened internal critic, who was angry at her for feeling sad and ashamed of her for feeling frustrated.

The "I'll Tell You How It Is" School of Happiness

The "I'll tell you how it is" school of happiness operates primarily in the realm of the second tier. It is less concerned with controlling our life situation and more interested in managing our experience of life. It attempts to empower us by taking control of the thoughts and feelings we have *about* our life. Reframing, rationalizing, seeing the glass half-full, and choosing our destiny are all courses taught in this program. If our real experience is something less than pleasurable, we can manage that experience, shapeshift it into something that allows us to maintain our sense of okay-ness. The idea is to make sure that we experience life in the right way so that

we can remain happy and avoid contact w
resemble un-happiness.

Let's say that our situation is that w
wanted, and that our experience of not gett
This particular self-help school believes tha
piness are incompatible. Thus, our experienc
to become something other than what it is
happiness must align with an emotional exp
The *thought police* are then dispatched. Unde
actually a good thing that we didn't get the jol
that challenge always makes us work harder. It i
because it's probably not the right job for us any
getting turned down will free us up for a job v
preciated, which certainly wouldn't be the case
didn't get! As it turns out, frustration is the wro
should be happy about getting passed over. This s
ness teaches us how to manage our experience, ho
should ourselves into feeling good. We decide wha
then we implement it.

Reframing is in fact a very helpful skill; we *do* wa
to see the light in what feels like a dark situation. Th
not that this system asks us to add a voice of positivity o
but rather, in how we accomplish this and what we do
to—the feelings that existed before.

For this school of thought, any negativity that is let
re-shaped into positivity is dangerous and has the potent
stroy us. We are not taught to gently add the positive to ou
world, but rather to violently bulldoze the residual negati
ings. The search for happiness in this system is a search f
dimensionality—all good.

The secret to well-being lies in the capacity to include and
within the layers of both the positive and the negative, to be
to tolerate the difficult experience and still experience the poss

realize now that it's not really me that it's happening to. What a relief. This me thing, this marriage thing and this argument thing are all just illusions." While my sangha-brother's words are true at the deepest level, and very helpful when applied in the appropriate framework, these same words can be misused and misunderstood. We can get stuck in a detached, observer role—separate from life— imagining that not caring and/or not feeling is the same thing as well-being and spiritual freedom. When the relationship we build with our own experience is one of pure observation, when detachment is the destination, we may have found a temporary relief from life, but we have not arrived at nor are we headed toward well-being.

The Topic of Medication

I am not about to debate the benefits and risks of anti-depressant medicine; this is its own topic and a different book. As a psychotherapist and spiritual advisor, I have watched people who have been stuck in despair and darkness for their entire lives released from suffering in a matter of a few weeks as a result of medication. I have worked with patients who were unable to move forward in their lives, but with the addition of anti-depressants, became unstuck and were able to create new possibilities. Medicine can offer miracles, and in some cases, it is the only way to create change. Working with people who have been dealt the horror of depression, it is clear that spiritual practice is not sufficient in relieving this disease, and I am deeply grateful to be able to offer those who suffer with depression a way to alter their unfortunate brain chemistry.

The merits of medicine, properly used, are inarguable. And yet, medicine is not always properly employed. Medicine can be used in a way that works against our awareness, and that keeps us locked in our addiction to happiness and fearful of anything other than happiness. Medication can be used as another technique to keep ourselves happy—perpetually liking the contents of our life, and dreading its alternative.

When Thomas came to see me he was worried. He had recently seen his general physician for a checkup, during which he was asked how he was doing overall in his life. After Thomas shared that he felt down about a recent breakup, his father's serious illness, and the long winter, his doctor suggested that Thomas consider going on Wellbutrin, an anti-depressant and seasonal affective disorder drug. Luckily, Thomas was alert and aware enough to be surprised and concerned by his doctor's suggestion, and that was when he reached out to me.

We use anti-depressants in this culture as a way to not feel the un-happiness that is a part of life, to bypass the healthy, appropriate responses we have to life's ups and downs. Breakups and illnesses are a part of being human. We need to be able to feel the heartbreak of our losses in order to heal from them, and also to be able to experience the joys of our blessings.

When we rush to medicate and *correct* our sadness, fearful and ashamed of any state *less* than happiness, we reinforce the belief that we cannot be okay when our life situation is not okay, cannot be well when un-happy feelings are present, and that any un-happiness, even when warranted, needs to be corrected—unaware that un-happy feelings serve us and have a place in the healing process.

Thomas and his female partner had broken up just two months prior to my meeting him. She had been an important relationship in his life. His father's illness was slow and terminal; he had been deteriorating for eighteen months. Thomas's sadness was appropriate to what was happening in his life. He was present with what was actually true, and within a healthy time frame for grief. It was clear to me that Thomas did not need to medicate his less-than-happy feelings. In fact, he expressed wanting to feel them. Thomas wanted an invitation into—and company for—his sadness, rather than a way around it. In the end, being able to experience his un-happiness was what allowed Thomas to walk through the next year of his life in which difficulty was the norm, and to do so fully awake and fully alive.

A year later, he expressed the following: "Being able to feel what I was feeling, to tolerate it, is what allowed me to be in the room with my Dad as he died, and to really be there with him. It was like being with the truth of this whole human beauty and tragedy—love. You helped me find a place to stand in the midst of the grief and that place gave me the strength to be there for, and with him at the end."

WELL-BEING BEGINS HERE

All of our approaches to creating happiness contain pieces of wisdom. Crafting our lives the way we want them to be is a good thing. We should strive to include the positive and reframe our negative experiences. We benefit by taking what works and leaving the rest behind. We need to be able to witness our own thoughts and feelings. When grief is overwhelming, sometimes we need a fast way out, just to help us get back on our feet.

But, we need more than these useful techniques—the medication, the Witness Protections . . . etc.—more than what these systems offer. We need a Plan B for when we cannot create the life situation that we want. We need guidance for those times when we know how we *should* or *want* to feel but can't bring ourselves to actually feel that way. Unfortunately, all of these schools of happiness abandon us when we cannot work their system, cannot control our life or how we feel about our life, cannot maintain our disinterest in our own life.

Well-being begins where these other schools leave off. Well-being can coexist with happiness, but does not rely on it. Well-being offers us a place to reside inside ourselves, a place where we can be okay when happiness is not available.

Christopher described himself to me as "a superstar." At the age of seventy, he had succeeded at everything in his life. He earned the top position in a financially successful corporation that was also known for its philanthropic work around the world. He was a star athlete who ran marathons and completed iron-man triathlons. He had a lovely wife, two wonderful sons who had attended the best colleges and graduate schools in the country, a sailboat, and a dog—the whole American enchilada. His life, to date, had been a truly happy one. But then something happened that was not in the plan. He got Parkinson's disease.

When the disease was first diagnosed, Christopher went to his board of directors and informed them of his condition. He was still in great shape and he would approach the Parkinson's as he had everything else in his life—as a winner. He was not ashamed of the diagnosis and all systems remained on full throttle. He could accomplish his work and run his marathons, everything that he derived his happiness from was still readily available to him. But, as disease has a way of doing, slowly, the Parkinson's started to take away the situations that created his happiness.

Christopher was not as able to be an athlete, to sail his boat, or train for his triathlons. As the medications caused him to slow down, it was not as easy for him to fulfill the role of CEO. While his thinking was still clear, he could no longer keep the hectic "around-the-world" schedule he had so loved. As his body began to shake, stiffen, and contort into strange shapes, he began to feel shame. His identity as a superstar, the image of himself that had also been a big part of his happiness, was deteriorating.

"If I can't be the golden boy, I can't live," he said on that first day we met, his head in his hands. Christopher was in crisis. He was being stripped of all the external situations as well as the self-image on which his happiness depended. If happiness could no longer be attained, which clearly it could not, he didn't see any possibility other than hell. He had not shared this with his family but suicide had become an option. When we began our work together, Christopher was managing his experience of the Parkinson's by hiding it. Not only did he hide his physical symptoms from all those he worked with, and sometimes even his wife, but also he hid his despair and his terror. His own experience of what he was living had become another assault to his crumbling self-image.

"If anyone sees that I am not managing this well, that the medicine is not working, that I am afraid and defeated, then I won't be that guy anymore," Christopher said.

"Are you that guy anymore?" I asked gently.

He paused, taking in my question. "Yeah, I know, but I still need them to think I am. It's all I've got. At least I can hang onto that for a little while longer. After that, I don't know. And Alison, my wife; my kids . . . she needs me to be the guy she married, they need me to be their Dad."

Christopher then told me a long story about one of his corporate coups, a gigantic success he had orchestrated despite no other guy being able to figure out the challenge. It was one of his finest glories in a life of glory. I listened with rapt attention, knowing that it was important that *I* know that he was *that guy*.

In the only way he knew how, Christopher was trying to hang onto his happiness and his identity. If he couldn't do the things that provided him with positive feelings, at least he could pretend that he could still do them—because the drizzle of self-esteem that he reaped from others' false beliefs about who he *was* was all that he had to hang onto, to save him from incurable darkness.

Christopher had an excruciating and challenging opportunity before him. He could not *do* his life the way he used to. If he did choose to stay alive, he would have to build a new place inside, one that could stand to be okay without all the pleasures that life had generously offered him, which could be okay even in the company of profound grief; he would need to know an internal presence that did not shame or judge him, but rather could be compassionate and understanding with the losses that were now a part of his experience. His task was to get to know himself in an entirely new way, a way that he most certainly would not choose if given the chance to coast out of life happily, as "a superstar." He had the opportunity (although he would not see it this way) to meet his real self, the self that was far larger and more infinite than the small self of accomplishments and pleasures that he had spent the last seventy years imagining himself to be. After seven decades of a happy life, a life well-lived, he had the chance, the imperative even, to get to know real well-being, and it was toward this place that we urgently embarked.

Despite our denials, happiness is often out of our control and temporary. Programs that promise to create and sustain it are inherently flawed. It was Christopher's body that got in the way of his being able to hold onto happiness, but we are all *Christophers* in one form or another. We are all presented with challenges that force us, again and again, to let go of our strategies for happiness—because we can't stay the same, because the river of life moves on and we cannot survive in the same way. We are all forced at various times to do without the contents of a pleasurable life, without the elements that offer us a good time. We are all—every one of us—headed into rough waters in this lifetime. It is not just at the end, when illness and loss enter the picture, that we find ourselves unable to make our situation pleasurable, or to manifest the ingredients of an existence that feels good. It is a continual event throughout life, sometimes more present and sometimes less, but always a part of being alive for everyone who was, is, and will ever be born.

2 TAKING CARE OF OURSELVES

Given the fact that we are consistently failing at achieving happiness, or rather, that happiness is consistently failing us by proving to be unsustainable, it is clear that we need to shift our life goal. Instead of chasing happiness, we need to discover well-being and the contentment that is part and parcel of that. Well-being/contentment is a larger and more reliable destination: not something to accomplish, but rather, something we need to uncover within ourselves. It is our true and natural resting state. Well-being/contentment is a practical goal for a life, a state that can survive and even thrive within the full range of situations that real life includes. Unlike happiness, well-being is always available and can exist within any external conditions. It does rely on one condition however, namely, that we be able to relate to our own experience with an attitude of kindness and curiosity.

There is one question I consistently ask myself, my clients, my friends, my family, and anyone else who might listen. It is a simple question: "How would you treat yourself if you were someone you actually loved?" This question serves to illuminate the giant chasm that exists between the manner in which we take care of ourselves, our own feelings, and the way we might take care of our child, a friend, or even a stranger. The truth is that we are not skilled at taking care of ourselves. In fact, we are quite inept.

Our parents (or primary caretakers) teach us how to parent ourselves. Our parents are our models. We soak in their attitude toward our feelings. We watch the way our parents interact with their own experience, how they self-parent. All of this information then becomes the blueprint for our own self-treatment. The style in which our parents parent our feelings becomes our gauge for how we deserve to be treated and how we set up our internal environment.

We come into this world with an inborn caretaker. We are our own friends—until we learn otherwise. And unfortunately, we do learn otherwise. In many families, we learn that our instinct for proper self-care, the care of our own truth, may not be the smartest or most adaptive behavior. It may not be safe for us to be in touch with our true feelings. As children, we need our parents to love us and keep us physically safe. These are our primary needs and all else will be sacrificed to make sure these needs are met. If our truth contains the potential to jeopardize our primary needs, as in "I don't like the way Mommy or Daddy makes me feel," it is our truth, rather than our mommy or daddy, that will be abandoned.

Furthermore, without the encouragement and support of our caretakers, it may not be possible for us to even know our authentic experience. Our experience, what we think, feel, and sense, is like a seed that needs to be watered and nourished. If our experience is not supported or nurtured by an external source, we may not even know we have an experience at all, and it is unlikely that we will be able to develop a loving relationship with something that we do not know exists.

In part, we are unable to properly self-care because we do not know how to be present with difficult experience. We have not learned how to sit with our own feelings. We do not know what to do with our sadness, our anger, our frustration, our confusion, our— you name it. We do not know how to comfort our own suffering, or even keep it company.

As children, we are encouraged to get away from pain. Rather than being trained in how to stay with uncomfortable emotion, we are instructed in how to avoid and escape it. The truth is, we cannot avoid or escape difficult feelings. Consequently, we have not learned one of the most basic and necessary skills needed to live our life well.

Too many of us grow up with parents who cannot tolerate their own difficult feelings, and as a result, are unable to bear the difficult feelings of their children. Emotional discomfort creates anxiety, sadness, guilt, inadequacy, anger, fear, or some other experience these parents cannot tolerate inside themselves. They then relate to their children's upset as they do their own, with aggression, fear, impatience, or some other such unkindness or rejection. They have to do something with their child's upset, to make it go away, not only because they cannot stand to be with it in their child, but because they cannot stand what it evokes inside themselves. An anxious or unfriendly relationship with their child's experience thus becomes the norm.

This relationship is then compounded by our society's misguided belief that our job as parents is to make our children's negative feelings go away, that this is what it means to take care of our children. Under the guise of trying to be helpful, parents often cause the greatest harm. It is not a parent's job to force his/her child's difficult feelings to go away. Quite the contrary; it is a parent's job to show their child how to tolerate and comfort challenging feelings, to be able to live with and learn from them. It is most important that parents be able to be present with their children's difficult experience, to not be scared off or destroyed by it, to demonstrate that we can be okay even when situations, thoughts, and feelings are not okay.

The task of parents is to trust that their own okay-ness and strength in the face of challenge will allow (rather than force) their child's feelings to ease and heal. Sadly, when this behavior is not modeled for us, when we are surrounded by grownups who are threatened and overwhelmed by our negative feelings, we too learn to enter into fearful and unkind relationship with our own experience.

OUR INNER CARETAKERS

In order to discover well-being we must build a new kind of relationship with our experience. But before we can build this new relationship, we must first understand and unravel the relationship we are in. We must become aware of the internal caretakers now in residence within us—how they talk to us, comfort or don't comfort us, blame or support us, whether their input helps or hurts. We need to investigate what our inner caretakers are doing with and to our feelings. With greater awareness of our internal caretakers, we can begin building a friendly relationship with our own experience, and in the process, begin creating the possibility for well-being.

So how do we self-parent? Who are the *caretakers* that live inside us? While there are as many different kinds of inner-parents as there are human beings, a few show up more frequently than others. Meet the "parents."

The Blamer

What did you do to cause the problem?

You are crying because you fell down. The Blamer self-parent starts with "Damn you, you see what happens when you run too fast!" The Blamer is the parent who is the first to tell you why you are the cause of whatever bad thing happened, to blame for whatever is upsetting you. So too, the Blamer is there to take the other guy's side, always quick with a reason for why he/she was entitled to do what he did to you. When my friend Marilee told me about not getting invited to a party she very much wanted to attend, it was her fault-finding inner-parent who relayed the story to me, and in the process, made it clear that Marilee's hurt was not of my concern.

"I probably didn't do anything to warrant an invitation," she said nastily. "I mean, why would they invite me? It's not like I ever gave a party and invited them! It's not like I have gone out of my way to be particularly friendly. In fact the last time I saw them I was in a rush and don't think I even said hello!"

When the Blamer is our internal self-parent, the relationship we build with our own feelings is critical and nasty. Since we are to blame for whatever bad thing has happened, our feelings about what happened are not welcome and certainly not deserving of attention or kindness. When we blame ourselves or take the other guy's side we are effectively invalidating our own experience and robbing ourselves of the right to our own support.

Mike, a sweet, intelligent, earnest young drummer was crazy about Pamela. "Every day I have to pinch myself that a woman like her actually chose me," he told me. They had been dating for about six months when she invited him up to her family home in Nantucket. He was nervous and excited, thrilled to be with her and to be included in her family, whom he had heard so much about. Pamela was from a big and important mainline brood, wealthy and sophisticated, and very close. She had attended the best schools and was certainly well-heeled. Mike, on the other hand, had grown up in Brooklyn with a single, alcoholic, emotionally abusive father in a roach-infested home. "A swan and a rusty wrench," was how he put it. While their backgrounds were very different, each saw something wonderful in the other. They had met at a performance of Mike's band and been together, he thought happily, since that first meeting.

Everything went wrong during that weekend visit. Mike sensed that Pamela was keeping her distance, and at a barbecue on Saturday evening a young man showed up whom Mike knew instinctively was in a relationship with Pamela. "The way she looked at him was unmistakable," he said, choking back tears. It turned out that his instincts were correct and, as dusk fell, Pamela informed Mike that she was indeed in a relationship with this other man and had been, even throughout her and Mike's six months together. She tried to console him with the fact that she had grown up with this boy and that he had always been her real sweetheart. She wanted Mike to know that her choice was not because of any failing on his part.

When Mike and I met on Monday, I was excited to hear about the trip, but I could see that he was in a terrible state, slumped into his chair. What broke my heart however, even more than hearing what Mike had lived through with Pamela, was what Mike was enduring at the hands of his own inner-parent. I was about to meet Mike's father—as he lived in Mike. The young man spent the next hour explaining why it all made sense that Pamela, a woman he loved, could not possibly love him.

The people in Pamela's family actually wanted to be together. Mike had never had that experience. For him, dinner was something to get through without being humiliated or having a bottle thrown at his head. In this family, they lingered at meals, and were interested in knowing each other. As he described, "I never knew that family could be like that. Like you actually want to see each other. That was a first for me." But instead of feeling compassion for how lacking his own family life had been, and how much he longed for a family like Pamela's, his own suffering became the target of his firing range. "And so it makes perfect sense that she would not want someone like me. I don't have that whole family thing, it's just not a part of me—something else I'm missing. How could she want me? A person who doesn't have any experience of family that is positive is damaged goods. Yuck... I get it."

Right there, where the opportunity for compassion and kindness appeared, in the truth of Mike's not getting to have a loving family, in the loss of the cherished relationship, was precisely where his blaming self-parent swooped in to do his *parenting*. There, where the wound needed caretaking was precisely where the Blamer self-parent poured the poison.

The Taskmaster

What are YOU going to do to fix it?

The Taskmaster inner-parent is a close relative of the Blamer, but rather than blame you for the event that caused your feelings to be hurt, this inner-parent assigns you a to-do list to fix the situation that is causing you upset. Since you are responsible for fixing the situation, the implication is that you are also to blame for what happened. While this parent is subtler than the Blamer in his/her presentation, the message is the same.

Since I had known Lynn (which was a long time), she had been aching for a romantic relationship. Each week, the same six of us met on our mats, yoga buddies. One by one, Lynn watched as each of us fell in love, got married and at least three of us had children, all while she remained unhappily single, frantically searching the on-line dating sites, but with no luck. At last, Lynn was dating someone she really enjoyed. She was so excited to finally have a boyfriend whom she actually liked, and who really liked her too. It was the first time a relationship felt mutual, and a very happy time in her life. One day, out of the blue, the man she was dating told her that he was not attracted to her and never really had been. While he liked her fine, he didn't like her enough to be his primary relationship. She did not have the body that he wanted, or so she reported, and there was nothing she could do about it.

Lynn felt blind-sided, frustrated, and heartbroken. Nonetheless, her Taskmaster inner-parent threw her under the proverbial bus, and bullied her heart right out of the dialogue. "Well obviously I have to get to the gym," she said matter-of-factly. "That's all there is to it. I mean can you blame him? I think I have been twice this year. I have to get this sack of lard into shape or no one will ever want me. Would you want these thighs? To begin with, I am going to stop eating all carbs and maybe just cut out dinner altogether. Actually I am going to start tonight so this is going to turn out to be just the kick in the ass, literally, that I need."

It was painful to watch as Lynn unknowingly rejected and battered her own feelings. Instead of a shoulder to lean on, Lynn's inner parent offered her a list of things she now had to do to make herself feel better. The implication being that if she did not spring into action, she would never get to have anything good in her life, or find relief from the pain she was in. After hearing from her inner-parent, she felt just as terrible, but now on top of her despair, she also felt anxiety and guilt—for all the things she had done wrong and all the things she needed to do to stop feeling this way. Rather than comforting her experience, her inner caretaker had contributed to her suffering.

With this type of inner-parent, the relationship with our own experience is one of abandonment and rejection. We are not interested in hearing from our experience, but only in fixing it and making it go away. If this self-parent offers our experience anything, it is a shot of fear and self-loathing. Lynn callously bypassed her grief and outrage without a second look, *invisibilized* her experience and went straight to her fix-it list.

Buried in the abandonment and rejection of her experience laid a strong element of self-blame. Her thighs were her fault, and with thighs like that, how could she imagine that she could ever be lovable? She had created her heartbreak and thus it was hers to fix. This was the real message she received from her inner-parent. Lynn deserved a list of responsibilities to change her situation, but certainly not any kindness for the experience that, after all, she had created. I hoped that she might be able to use her list as a tissue for her tears, but by the time she had completed her recipe for repentance, she no longer felt deserving of even a tissue.

The Blamer Junior

Stop feeling the way you do!

While the Blamer Junior is a relative of the original Blamer, the subject of his/her blame is different. This is the parent who tells you that the way you feel about a situation is the wrong way to feel. Your experience is incorrect. As opposed to the self-parent who tells you that you caused the event that led to your upset, this inner-parent tells you that you are to blame for your feelings *about* the situation.

A colleague, Frank, was hoping to be invited to join the Inner Circle Committee, the group of top executives hand-picked from various departments whose job it was to make the most important strategic decisions for the company. As it turned out, he was not selected. When Frank shared this, he was visibly bothered, seemingly angry, and definitely hurt. But soon after, his Blamer Junior inner-parent showed up. Immediately, his tone and body language shifted and he began telling me that it was his sensitivity that was the problem, and probably the reason why he was not selected in the first place. He was overly-sensitive and weak and "nobody wanted that kind of mess on their committee." The fact that Frank cared so much was humiliating. "I will never be a top player if I can't get rid of this sensitivity," he told me, angrily. His feelings about being passed-over were the enemy.

It may be that we are too sensitive or wrong for even being upset. It may be that we only look at the negative side and are unappealingly pessimistic. It may be that we have a problem with everyone and this is just another in our long list of gripes. But whatever the criticism of our response is, the take-away is that we are flawed, and this is why we are in the situation we are in.

With Blamer Junior as our inner-parent, we learn the same lesson, to aggressively reject our own experience. Our experience is the enemy since it is what creates the problem. But what are we to do when the enemy is within, when our experience is to blame for our suffering? How to get away from our own experience? Certainly with this as the goal, we build a relationship of fear, resentment, and avoidance with our own feelings. Our experience is not something to befriend, it is a dangerous traitor—incompatible with our happiness.

The Pseudo-Realist

That's not really how you feel.

Once again, with this inner-parent taking care of us, our experience is the problem, albeit with a slightly different twist. This is the inner-parent who continually reminds us of what is true, what we should feel, and why our actual experience is not real.

Lina hailed from an affluent high-society family, one that was well known and very generous in New York philanthropic circles. She was raised to be a concert violinist. While she was highly talented musically, she suffered with anxiety and panic attacks when she had to perform. There was tremendous pressure on her to be brilliant and to serve as a representative of the family's importance. Indeed the family's grandiosity balanced perilously on Lina's little shoulders. Lina (and her nervous system) most definitely felt the pressure. When she told her mother that she was anxious, her mother explained that little girls didn't get anxious. Everybody at the concert loved her, and there was no reason for her to feel anxious. Because of all these good reasons, Lina could not really be nervous. Now that's a confusing message, particularly because she did feel nervous!

With this inner-parent, what we feel is not only incorrect, but also not real because it does not align with what makes sense or is reasonable to others. As a result, we are to replace our actual experience with the one that we *should be* having. The consequence of this is that we build a relationship with our experience that is distrustful and rejecting. We learn to invalidate our feelings since they are unreliable and do not match with what is *true*. Our experience is something that needs to be turned off or at least corrected, but clearly not something to be acknowledged or consoled.

The Scorekeeper

What difference will it make?

"Why bother feeling bad about it?" asks this inner parent. "It's already done, water under the bridge." If we did not get the job and they already hired someone else, it is pointless to feel bad about the situation or waste any kindness on ourselves. The situation is already over. In this self-parent's system, compassion is a zero sum commodity, not to be doled out without an achievable purpose. If expressing our experience cannot change the situation (externally) then any more time spent with it is self-indulgent and futile. This inner-parent is interested only in results.

The relationship we then build with our experience is either demanding (it must exist for a purpose) or dismissive. Our feelings must accomplish something in order to justify their existence or be considered valid. Unfortunately, the task our feelings have been assigned to accomplish is not an appropriate one. Being compassionate with our experience will probably not get our job back, but it will benefit us by making us feel better. With this self-parent in residence, our experience is valued only if it can produce something in the world that is deemed important. Our experience, on its own, is of no inherent value and is treated accordingly.

The Justifier

Think about it from his perspective!

This inner-parent is always quick to point out why the other guy is justified in doing what he did to us. When Alison told her mom that her fifth grade teacher had walked out of the room just as she started her big presentation (on which she had worked all year), her mom reminded Alison how hard it must be for teachers to sit in one place all day long, and pointed out that even teachers have to use the bathroom every once in a while, just like Alison. Alison remembered feeling guilty for not thinking of it from Mrs. Anderson's perspective—how selfish she had been to actually feel entitled to her upset. As she said, "I had been thinking only of my own feelings!"

When Alison informed her grandmother that her teenage boyfriend had broken up with her because he wanted to date other people, her grandmother remarked that it was a good thing that young people didn't get serious so early, and that Alison's now ex-boyfriend must be a wise young fellow. "Think about it from his perspective: a young handsome man, why would he want to put all his eggs in one basket at this age?"

When Alison told her aunt that she had been passed over for the job she wanted and that they had hired someone more junior in the company, her aunt responded, "You both will do a good job, but they can pay her less for the same work. From where they sit, it makes sense for them to promote her, doesn't it?"

For weeks, Alison had been telling me how her children's nanny was refusing to do the job that she was hired to do. She had stopped cleaning the girls' bedrooms or doing laundry, complaining that it made her back hurt. She had stopped cleaning the rest of the house, explaining that she was too tired. The nanny was demanding the same pay, but only doing the parts of the job that she enjoyed. As a result, Alison was doing her own job (out of the house) as well as the nanny's chores inside the house. She was paying the nanny to have a good time with her children while she herself never got to see them. In her words: "I am on my knees scrubbing the bathroom floor and I hear Marta and my kids giggling on the couch."

"Think about how hard it is for Marta," Alison repeated over and over again. "A single mother without great English skills, and without a community. You can understand why her back hurts. She is probably carrying her baby around all night. I would not want to do laundry either—if I were her!" Alison kept reminding me why her experience did not matter, and most importantly, why Marta's behavior was justified. Not surprisingly, Alison was a perfect member of the team of women who had raised her.

The Justifier inner-parent teaches us that our experience is not important. Our hurt does not matter. *We* do not matter. Confusingly, however, other people's hurt does matter, a great deal in fact. Experience matters too, but only when it belongs to the other. In place of comfort, our experience is offered an explanation of why the situation makes sense, and consequently why our experience is un-deserving of kindness or attention. And with that explanation, we get fed an additional dose of guilt, for even imagining that what we were living might have mattered.

The Neglecter

Just go away.

The Neglecter inner-parent turns his/her back on our feelings altogether, effectively invisibilizing our experience. Our experience is simply not important enough to notice or inquire about—much less befriend. As a result of this neglect, we build no relationship with our experience whatsoever; it does not exist as there is nothing and no one to be in relationship with. Eventually, we stop even knowing what we feel, or who we are.

∾

Each of these inner-parents, regardless of their particular method of caretaking, is responsible for creating a specific kind of damage. Over time, the mistreatment, distortion, and neglect of our experience causes us to lose contact with our true feelings. We stop knowing how or where to find our authentic experience. This loss of contact with our own experience is perhaps the worst of all the damage that improper self-parenting creates.

CONNECTING TO THE TRUTH OF OURSELVES

Eleanor relayed the following story, aptly demonstrating what it looks like when the tether to our truth gets disconnected. The family was scheduled to drive out of town for a wedding. Eleanor had made the household preparations and arranged the details for the trip, which were numerous. On the way back from the playground the morning of their trip, Eleanor's daughter had thrown a ferocious temper tantrum in the hallway of their apartment building. The little girl did not want to go inside and was unrelenting in her obstinacy. This was a regular event with her daughter, and with only a half-hour to go before their departure time, Eleanor did not have time to sit with her daughter until she calmed down (a process that often took more than an hour). Instead, Eleanor picked her daughter up and physically brought her into the apartment against her will, with the tantrum now becoming a violent rage. As she was prying the child's fingernails from her calf muscle, Eleanor watched the neighbor's door open just a crack, wide enough for her neighbor, "the perfect Mom," to cast her disapproving eyes over Eleanor, like "a cloth of shame." In the meantime, the neighbor offered no assistance, not even a supportive smile.

When Eleanor finally managed to drag her daughter into the apartment, her husband was there in the living room on his BlackBerry, busily texting and working on the computer despite full awareness of their departure time. He had not showered and was nowhere near ready to leave. Their son sat next to him in pajamas, covered in crumbs, watching cartoons, despite her having asked her husband to get him ready to leave. Upon seeing their state of unreadiness, Eleanor inquired about her husband's plan as they were already behind schedule. Martin, her husband, did not respond, and never glanced up from his screen. She repeated her question, this time with more urgency and irritation, tears now escaping from the corners of her eyes. Again he ignored her, which had become his habit when she needed or wanted something from him.

Ironically, it was Eleanor who was left feeling anxious, guilty, and terrible about herself. "I obsessed the whole car ride to the wedding about what an impossible and difficult person I am, how anyone could bear someone as crazy as me." In her estimation, she was an abusive mother, having dragged her child into the apartment without spending the time to reason with her, without any compassion for her tantrum. (In fact she had reasoned with her for some time before picking her up and bringing her inside the apartment, but she had forgotten that part.) She was a nagging and crazy wife, always riding her husband about something or other, pestering him about nothing. "Why can't I just leave him alone and let him be?" Furthermore, she informed me that, as her friend, I needed to help her conquer her neurotic anxiety, because after all, look what it was doing to everyone around her (including me, she was sure!).

I asked Eleanor what I thought was a simple question: what had the morning been like—for her. Interestingly, the question seemed to profoundly irritate her. Perhaps she sensed that my question suggested that her own experience might be something different than her self-judgments or the perceived negative judgments of others. She again recounted her crimes, as if to remind or convince me of her badness. She had full access to her blaming inner-parent's criticisms, but nowhere in her response was *her own* experience of what had happened. Her inner-parent had not only kidnapped her experience, but worse, had disconnected the pathway that connected her to her truth, the pathway to that internal place where her real feelings might have formed.

Eleanor did not know how to answer my question—how else she could feel besides her habitual self-loathing. She felt frustrated, defeated, and now inadequate as well, for failing to feel something about what had happened other than what she had already reported.

With a sprinkling of humor, hoping that her truth would recognize itself somewhere in my words, I exploded the proverbial kitchen sink. I told her how frustrating and upsetting I personally thought her daughter's behavior was, how maddening the continual tantrums, how relentless the demands, how impossible to control, and finally, how exhausting to have to be a patient and loving mother at every minute, even when all I would want to do is get on the next plane to anywhere! How much I admired her for not pulling her own hair out, or her daughter's! And as for her neighbor, I offered that I had personally joined my apartment's coop board just to keep the *Betty Crockers* off the premises, that if the *perfect moms* of the world were not going to help us regular moms in desperate times, that we sure didn't need them as our neighbors!

Without pausing for a rebuttal, I moved on to her husband. How infuriating to be ignored when what she was trying to do was take care of everyone, including him. How frustrating and hurtful to be deliberately shut out. How unfair to turn this wedding of their mutual friend, something that he had claimed he *wanted* to attend, into something that *she* was dragging him to. How dare he! And as for her son, the little bugger, how challenging he was, always forcing her into the role of *bad cop*, making her repeat everything at least a dozen times before he even began to listen. Imagine, eight years on the planet and still completely unable to take responsibility for any of his own affairs! With intention, I went full out with my commentary!

As I confessed the feelings that *I* might have experienced that morning, her eyes came alive. Without much effort, she was able to recognize her own experience, to claim what sat beneath all the self-judgments. She did indeed have feelings, not deeply buried and not mild ones, as it turned out—feelings quite different than the self-blame, responsibility, and guilt that she had so readily offered as a stand-in for her experience. In hearing my assessment of her morning, an infinite well of truth came into being. It had been unformed but now took shape. With delight, I met my friend Eleanor's anger, exasperation, outrage, bafflement, fed-up-ness, disappointment, confusion, hurt, longing, loneliness, and despair. I guess you could say that I met Eleanor, period. And by the end of our conversation, she had found a tether into her own truth, a connection to what she had lived that awful morning. Glimpsing a self and an experience that existed underneath and separate from her inner parent's judgments of her, Eleanor was starting to get a feel for what I meant when I asked, "How was it for *you*?"

Given the damage that our self-parents inflict, it is counterintuitive to consider that somewhere in each of them is a misguided desire to try to lessen our suffering. And yet, at some level, these inner-parents are trying to change our negative experience into something more positive, or at the very least, to lessen or avoid our pain. Unfortunately, the methods they use are deeply flawed and end up adding more suffering to the suffering that is already there.

MISGUIDED EMPOWERMENT

When Marilee takes the blame for not getting invited to the party, she is, ironically, trying to empower herself, to feel less hurt. Blaming herself for her rejection makes her feel less rejected. If she is *un-invitable*, the party-giver did not actually exclude her. Hurting herself feels better and less humiliating than having someone else hurt her. *I can hate myself far more than you will ever hate me* is actually an effort, albeit a misguided one, to protect ourselves from the sting of another's rejection. Since Marilee does not understand why she was not included, the experience feels unfair and confusing. But by taking the blame for her exclusion, what happened now makes sense and the unfairness and confusion are eradicated. The attempt to feel better is there—to correct her experience of powerlessness, humiliation, and unfairness. However, the system fails as Marilee simply replaces one set of bad feelings with another, and her authentic experience ends up festering below a fresh batch of negative self-judgments, with no space to shift or heal.

Similarly, by responding to her upset with a list of ways to make herself more appealing, Lynn's Taskmaster inner-parent is trying to empower her and eradicate her experience of helplessness after her boyfriend's incomprehensible dismissal. In a backhanded way, she is trying to offer herself a way out of pain. Like Marilee, the experience of powerlessness, frustration, and suffering is what Lynn is trying to escape. And indeed, it is not the improvement lists that are the problem; we need to know there is a way out of pain. But once again, the problem is that Lynn's experience of the situation— the hurt, anger, and helplessness—are not consoled nor offered any space to heal. Her experience is shoved into a gym bag. While temporarily relieving and empowering, in the end, this approach does not provide the help it intends.

In both the Blamer Junior (*Stop feeling the way you do!*) and Pseudo-Realist (*That's not really how you feel*) self-parents, there is a similarly misguided effort to help get us out of pain. If our experience is not desirable, these methods seek to make the un-happy feelings go away, to criticize, bully, or shapeshift our experience into something desirable, or at the very least, bearable.

Frank does not want or even know how to feel his sense of loss about being excluded from his company's inner circle. But he does know how to berate himself, and is quite skilled at feeling guilty. By attacking himself, Frank turns his experience into something familiar and that he knows he can tolerate. In the same vein, Lina's mother cannot tolerate the truth: her daughter is anxious. And so she does away with her child's anxiety and turns Lina's worry into something "unreasonable," which as her mother, she can bear. For the same reasons that the previous methods fail to help us heal, these fall short as well.

The Scorekeeper self-parent is not going to *go there*, into our feelings that is, unless the payoff warrants the suffering. By avoiding our feelings, the Scorekeeper is trying to keep us away from what it perceives as dangerous and painful. He/she is trying to keep us from experiencing loss—unless there will be gain to make up for it. Unfortunately, we need permission to *go there*, into our feelings, to know that we can be safe *there* too, and most of all, to heal.

The Justifier self-parent wants us to empathize with the other person, to understand why he did what he did, even though it hurt us. The belief is that if we understand that there is a good reason for what he did, we will not be hurt. In validating the perpetrator's actions and intentions, this inner-parent is trying to convince us that the other person did not mean to hurt us, and consequently, we need not feel bad.

And yet, understanding the reasonableness of the other's behavior does not lessen our hurt. If anything, it makes us feel worse, as the caring that we so crave is offered to the other guy. The situation makes sense and the other guy was right to do what he did, but there's nobody on our side, no empathy for our experience—which we need. So too, the Justifier, by implying that we should not be hurt, ends up invalidating the hurt that is already there. Despite his/her good intentions, we walk away from this inner-parent with more pain than we started with.

Finally, the Neglector self-parent. How could ignoring our feelings ever be imagined as helpful in any way? This inner parent believes that unseen feelings are unfelt feelings, that our experience—unaddressed—does not exist. Unfortunately, neglecting our experience does not make our experience not exist, nor does it save us from its pain. We can ignore our feelings, but they are still there. In truth, abandoning our experience leaves it hurt, stuck, angry, and once again, unhealed. The Neglector inner-parent's method for annihilating pain creates its own. Furthermore, when our experience is not worthy of attention, *we* are not worthy of attention—or being loved for that matter.

Although each of these bad self-parents wants to make our unhappiness and pain go away, they are unwilling to accompany us through our pain, and thus to help it heal—a different effort than making the pain go away. These inner *caretakers* refuse to include our experience—us—in the process of trying to save us from discomfort. With their help, we are taught to reject, abandon, ignore, judge, and mistreat ourselves. We are shown how to build a relationship of unkindness with our experience, which then, tragically, causes us to lose touch with our truth altogether. In the end, we are in the *care* of caretakers who are at best unskilled, and at worse, dangerously unkind.

3 FEAR OF OURSELVES

Why are we so unskilled at taking care of our own experience? How did we end up so misguided, aiming for happiness but living unhappily, and so far off course from well-being? Volumes have been written and still need to be written on the reasons for our predicament. Psychologists, sociologists, ministers, rabbis, anthropologists, economists, biologists, writers, and historians . . . every profession has weighed in with a theory on why we treat ourselves the way we do. As a therapist, however, I have learned that questions that begin with *why* do not heal, but rather, invite more intellectual dialogue. An interesting way to pass an afternoon perhaps, good cocktail conversation, but such questions do not generate fundamental change. Therefore, I will leave the *whys* on happiness and our self-treatment to others. My interest lies specifically in the *how-s*. How to shift our relationship with our experience, to move from blindness and unkindness to awareness and compassion? What do we need to learn to get off the wheel of happiness and suffering and become well?

Before we can begin changing our relationship with ourselves, we must first change our relationship with contradiction. Being able to tolerate internal contradiction is crucial to the development of well-being. We think in black or white, good or bad, happy or sad. And yet, life is always "both and." When two conflicting feelings are present at the same time, we use the word "but" to separate them, and then set out to do away with one or the other, as if our experience is an algebra problem that must resolve itself in a single answer. We need to replace the word "but" with the word "and." I feel happy and sad; my experience is both, equally, all at once.

Our attempt to make our experience one way is an effort to make our life understandable. Uncomfortable with complexity—the messiness of the internal landscape—we prefer that our emotions take the form of bullet points in a PowerPoint presentation, clean, clear, and bite-sized, and that all fall on the same side of the line. We are in an adversarial relationship with all those feelings that fall on what we consider the *wrong* side. But we are made of many parts and play many roles. Each of our parts and identities has its own wants, needs, and lived experience. This is not to say that we are all multiple personality types, just that there are contradictory wants and needs simultaneously within each of us.

In thinking about my daughter going to sleep-away camp for the first time, I feel a thousand contradictory emotions. As mommy, I feel profoundly heartbroken. The image of her little hand waving goodbye from behind the glass of the bus window, not getting to see her smile for a month. The irrevocable truth of time, little by little removing her from me, all sends me into a puddle on the floor. As the wife me, I feel quite excited and a bit anxious too. All this space without the kids to fill it up. As the professional me, there is delight and a great sense of freedom and opportunity. Three different, equally strong experiences of the same situation, all there at once. To discover well-being, we must become more comfortable with allowing all of our experiences to coexist simultaneously. With *and*, not *but*, as our guide, we can become curious about our internal contradictions. We can build an inclusive and welcoming relationship with each of our feelings, regardless of whether they agree or disagree with the others.

We talk a lot about self-care in this culture, but what does self-care really mean? For most people, self-care translates to getting a massage, making the time to eat lunch, taking a brisk walk, putting on our oxygen mask first. These are all valid self-caring actions for sure, but a deeper level of self-care exists that is not about externally *doing* for ourselves, but rather about internally *being* with ourselves in a manner that is kind. It is one thing to take ourselves out for lunch, but something else entirely and far more radical to honor and comfort our own feelings. This *being* variety of self-care not only is not encouraged, but often is prohibited, specifically, by fear. We are afraid of what will happen to us—who we will become—if we start caring about our own feelings, or just being kind to ourselves. So what are we so afraid of? What is it about developing a friendly relationship with ourselves that is so threatening?

Who Will I Become?

Selfish

Self-compassion is something that most of us would claim we possess. We *say* we care about ourselves. But in fact, when it comes to actually treating ourselves as someone we care about, now that is considered selfish. *How selfish of me to spend all that time thinking about me when so many people are suffering!* The fear of being judged (by oneself or others) as selfish is what keeps most people out of counseling, even when they desperately need it. As one woman who was decidedly not blessed with self-compassion complained, "It's always about me me me! Helping others is what makes us feel better!" Indeed, helping others does make us feel better but not if we are not helping ourselves as well.

We are afraid that if we care for ourselves, there won't be any caring left for others, as if caring were a finite commodity. If we take the time to pay attention to our own experience, we will become so self-involved that we will end up only interested in ourselves, so egotistical that we will stop wanting to ever be kind to anyone else. In this belief system, our caring for others is a façade of sorts, something we do to seem like a good person. Underneath it, we are only interested in ourselves and that truth must be kept rigorously in check.

We are desperately afraid of who we would become were we to treat ourselves with sweetness. And yet, it is only when we feel well taken care of, when our feelings have been properly heard and addressed that we have adequate resources to offer others. When our own well is full, we can experience our genuine desire to help others. Relating to ourselves with kindness actually increases our compassion and makes us less selfish.

Furthermore, when we are able to empathize with our own suffering, we can genuinely empathize with the pain of others. Conversely, when we reject our own feelings, we cannot be truly compassionate with others, certainly not to our full capacity, as a large part of our heart is closed off and inaccessible. This is not to say that we cannot be kind human beings without being kind to ourselves but, without the ability to relate lovingly with our own experience, we are severed from the real depth of our loving potential. It is as if we are living in a puddle when we could have access to the ocean.

Those of us who are so called *givers,* can fall into this trap with ease. We take care of everyone in our life and we like this role. But somehow we don't make it onto our own list of the deserving. It is important for us to realize that we are also human beings, to consider our experience as we would any other person's, to know that we too are deserving of basic kindness, the same kindness that we so readily offer to others. With this small but profound shift in awareness, our ability to love cracks open. Once our own suffering and longings matter, we are able to love with the true fullness of our being, ourselves included. While we may have thought we were already being loving with others, we now realize that we may not ever have been fully openhearted with them either. A fellow helping professional once confessed that she helped others because she liked the way she felt about herself when she was helping, but that she was not sure she knew how to actually care about others (and certainly not about herself).

When we know what loving attention actually feels like, when we can receive it from our own self, it is then that we can genuinely offer it to and for another creature. What we bring to others then arises out of our own compassionate heart, which includes compassion for ourselves—as just another living creature. What is remarkable too is that, in offering this kind of authentic loving attention, it is as if we are receiving it at the same time. As one friend expressed, "There is no separation between the two, the giver and the receiver. We are simply sharing one heart!" When our heart cracks open to our own experience, we benefit from helping others, but in an entirely fresh and generous way.

The rapidly exploding field of neuroscience provides further evidence for the link between self-kindness and kindness for others. There are now scientific studies coming from brain researchers like Richard Davidson, which show that meditation (which includes practicing compassion for oneself) actually develops the part of the brain that feels and expresses empathy.[1] Using magnetic resonance imaging, we can now concretely determine that empathy for our own experience builds our neurological capacity for caring. Being kind to our own feelings does not make us more selfish—it makes us kinder.

Lazy

After *selfish*, the second criticism that we usually attack ourselves with is *lazy*. As Janet, a student, stated, "If I were to build a friendly relationship with myself, I would end up lying on the couch all day with no motivation to ever move." We believe that the only way to make ourselves do anything is to use force, become our own dictators. Kindness toward ourselves will only lead to sloth. In this system, our basic nature is understood to be lazy and uninspired. Since action is contrary to our nature, it must be imposed against our will and with aggression. The danger in honoring our own feelings, supporting ourselves as we are, is that nothing will ever get done.

The link between self-care and sloth is a false one. In truth, when we have a friendly relationship with ourselves, when we can listen kindly to our own experience and take our own side, we are far more likely to act and take risks. If we know that when we fall, a friend will be there to catch us, we are more willing to get off the couch and take the leap. On the other hand, if our relationship with ourselves is aggressive and judgmental, we remain afraid to take chances because of how we will be treated if we fall short of our expectations. The fear of our own self-aggression is what prohibits our natural ability to act.

Interestingly, new neurological research also suggests that compassion meditation has an effect on our ability to take action. Studies now show that a regular meditation practice actually enlarges the part of the brain that stimulates action.[2] This speaks directly to our fear of laziness. When we are consistently compassionate with our own experience we are also developing our ability to act from that kindness, both for ourselves and others.

Never Change/Never Improve

Another false fear related to self-care is that being kind to ourselves will mean that we will always accept ourselves exactly the way we are, however that is, even if that is not a healthy way to be. In other words, self-care will keep us from growing or improving. Self-care will translate to a blind and passive surrender to however we are. In the deepest sense, a loving relationship with our experience does involve a kind of unconditional or radical acceptance of ourselves and our feelings as they are, but this does not mean that we stop wanting to improve, or that we are content to stop evolving. Our acceptance of who and how we are in the moment, the level that we have reached so to speak, forms the ground from which we want to grow. Acceptance and striving coexist simultaneously.

In fact, it is through our acceptance of our feelings *as they are* that we strengthen our natural instinct to improve. When we can allow ourselves to experience the suffering that results from our mistakes, our instinct to evolve naturally arises. Our feelings about our failings, when they are felt, actually generate a desire to change. We suffer when we fail and that suffering—if experienced—ignites our creative imagination, and indeed we find ways to improve.

On the other hand, when we are yelled at, ignored, or shamed for our mistakes, our own remorse and our natural desire to do it better never take form. Filled to the brim with criticism, our desire to grow has no space to bloom. We end up with a lot of negative judgments about ourselves and demands that we do it differently. And we may do it differently the next time, but not because we want to, but because we *should*. Any change in our behavior comes from the need to escape further attacks. *Should* may make things happen, but as a motivating force, it is never as powerful or creative as *want*. *Want* empowers us to change and can only be fueled by our truth.

Michael hailed from a lower middle-class family with lots of siblings; there were no presents for birthdays or other holidays. The one gift Michael did receive was a hand-me-down bicycle, a surprise gift from his cousin. Michael loved his bicycle more than anything he had ever owned. He repainted and detailed it with great care, spent hundreds of hours on it. When he wasn't in school, he was with his bicycle. It was his freedom, his independence, his lucky charm with the girls, his prize possession.

Returning from school one day, Michael rode up to the back porch and heard the phone ringing. He knew his father had been expecting an important call about a job and so Michael dropped his bike and ran inside to get the phone, nearly killing himself on the steps. After taking the message (from the possible employer) he was so excited to tell his dad that he forgot to bring his bicycle inside. The next morning it was gone and Michael was heartbroken. When his father found out why he was crying, he viciously tore into Michael, calling him a "moron" and a "good-for-nothing, ungrateful punk." His father expressed delight that "another moron would now get to have the rusty piece of junk." Michael had never forgotten his father's words, and particularly how he had called his beloved friend a piece of junk. For months, his father berated him for being stupid, irresponsible, and ungrateful. The message was clear: Michael did not deserve to have a bike. And indeed there were no more bicycles after that day.

Michael became a successful and organized man, certainly not someone you would call irresponsible. He talked about his life with a reserved and contained quality. He was not someone you would describe as spontaneous or joyful. He had lived his whole life not being irresponsible. In addition, he did everything to show that he was grateful for my caring. He thanked me often, regularly repeated how appreciative he was of my help. Nothing was left to chance. And yet, a quality in his appreciation always felt dry and forced, not false, but rather strained and imprisoned. He meant the things he said—I knew he was grateful—but his words did not seem to come from his heart. They didn't feel like genuine expressions of a gratitude that he could feel. While I did not know about the bicycle incident until later, I could not help but feel that his *good behavior* was just that, and mostly, an effort to avoid punishment.

After some time I offered my experience of Michael's sense of responsibility, with him, gently. It was then that he broke down in tears and shared the story of his bicycle. "God I loved Spencer, that was its name. I don't think I had ever loved anything like that bike. I was so proud of it. It made me cool. I was so grateful to have it, and I took such good care of it. I was excited for my father to get a job, which I knew we badly needed." There was no one who felt worse than Michael about having left the bike on the back porch. I sat silently with Michael as he sobbed twenty-seven-year-old tears.

For nearly three decades Michael had been carrying his feelings about what had happened. It was the experience that had never been allowed a seat at his own table. The suffering he experienced about having lost Spencer could finally be felt and heard. "I didn't mean to do it. I wouldn't have left it again," he kept repeating. These were life-changing days—both that day when he was fifteen and the day he finally owned his feelings about it, witnessed by me.

After that meeting, Michael's manner was more alive and free. He was still highly responsible, but his responsibility and appreciation had a different quality, as if emancipated, and emanating from a different place in him. Rather than trying to be a good boy, Michael had gained access to his real feelings of respect for our work. He was responsible because he wanted to be, because he felt the desire to honor our relationship. He had taken ownership of his own experience. He told me how grateful he was far less often, but when he did, it felt authentic—it was coming from his heart. Once his experience of grief and remorse had been heard, his organic sense of responsibility and gratitude could finally emerge. His goodness—and innocence—was known and no longer needed to be proven.

If Michael had been allowed to live the loss of his bicycle as a thirteen-year-old, he would not have left another one on the back porch. He would have been able to feel his own loss, to experience the sadness, and as a result would not have recreated the experience for himself. When our experience is offered the space to be heard and understood, when it is treated with the respect that it deserves, it, the experience itself, naturally and independently evolves and moves us toward growth.

Shame is a tough nut to crack. It is slow to change and usually melts over time rather than cracks. Shame sticks to us with a resilience that is stronger than perhaps any other emotion. It is a super-emotion in that, like a toxic gas, it seeps past temporary feelings, below temporary feelings, and sinks deep into the core of our identity. Given its strength, in order to ease shame we must be able to offer ourselves a kindness that is just as fierce and powerful, a warrior's kindness.

Sarah was buried in shame, primarily about her job performance. She had shot up the investment-banking ladder at lightning speed but, unbeknownst to her higher-ups, had avoided many of the responsibilities that her position required. A stack of documents hid under her desk, issues that she had neglected to address and whose deadlines had since passed. She lived in constant fear of being found out for her negligence, and being exposed as the imposter that she believed she was.

When I innocently inquired what sorts of tasks ended up in the pile under her desk, Sarah explained (with irritation) that they were the tasks that she could not make sense of, the ones that were "just too dreadful to get near." Some were tasks that she had tried to accomplish on her own but could not complete, while others she could not even understand how to begin. She was quick to let me know however, that all were tasks that she was capable of figuring out, "if she would just do it." It sounded to me like she had a lot on her plate that was beyond her understanding, and so I asked if there was a way that she could reach out for help, to one of her senior partners perhaps, for further clarification on the most complicated tasks.

It was at this moment that Sarah's expression changed and her inner-parent appeared, pouncing at the chance to humiliate her. "I am perfectly capable of figuring out these tasks," she said, exasperated by my ridiculous suggestion. "You don't get it, I am just lazy . . . I can't finish anything. That's why I have a pile under my desk that is going to get me fired." Sarah also told me that she was someone who had always avoided things when they got hard, who made decisions by not making decisions. The criticisms came fast and furious. In listening to her shame herself, it was clear that her behavior (which had continued over her entire career) had never been given the kindness, curiosity or emotional oxygen to change. We were not even allowed to inquire what her actual experience was, under the avoidance and attacks.

Persevering through her self-loathing, I asked Sarah if I could invite the *part* of her, the hand if you will, that hid the documents under her desk into the dialogue, if we could hear *its* experience. Even if she did not, I wanted to know that *part* of her, and understand what made it feel so afraid and helpless. Not surprisingly, her response came from her inner-parent, who reminded me that there was nothing Sarah could not figure out on her own. She was not as helpless as she was making it sound; I should not be fooled. Sarah was a failure when it came to facing challenges. This *caretaker* made sure that I knew that this was not an isolated event, but rather how Sarah operated in all the areas of her life.

Undaunted, I persisted in trying to befriend her experience. While she might be able to figure out these tasks intellectually, I said that there was still something in the way of her being able to actually get them done, and maybe whatever that was, was not about being able to figure them out. Perhaps that was something that we didn't know yet. In this way, I was trying to work with her inner-parent, to make him/her correct in a sense, agreeing that maybe Sarah could indeed figure out her tasks, but still this did not mean that she could complete them. Maybe we were all correct, but just missing some information.

This statement seemed to shift the mood, as if we had thrown her inner-parent a bone. My hope was that maybe now we could hear the faint whispers of the *part* of Sarah that felt helpless. Immediately, Sarah's body relaxed, and we sat quietly for a bit. I then asked if she could again ask that *part* of her that puts the documents under her desk, if *it* feels like these tasks are possible (even though she could certainly figure them out). She shook her head *no*. "*It* feels that they are impossible, like they are just too horrible to go anywhere near," she whispered. We were making progress. We had managed to get past her inner-parent's barricade of judgment. We were now sitting with her actual experience; her helplessness and confusion finally had been given permission to speak.

Over time I came to know Sarah's truth, her sense of inadequacy and paralysis, which had begun when she was a young child trying to manage a home-life that was beyond her ability—a task that truly was impossible. I came to know her helplessness, how she had never had anybody to turn to for help, how asking for help had led to shame and criticism for being incompetent and ignorant. Through her reflections, I met the parents who had raised her, who were unable to comfort or bear feelings of any kind. "'Get busy with something else. Distract yourself.' This was their best effort, and that was on a really compassionate day," she said, describing the care she had received.

Certain kinds of tasks, particularly those that are confusing and not immediately understandable, trigger strong fear and inadequacy in many of us. The state of *not knowing* can feel dangerous and threatening. When Sarah's efforts did not accomplish what she was supposed to deliver, when new strategies had to be created because the existing ones had failed, her self-loathing, terror of being unable, and inability to calm herself prevented her from moving forward. Because of her fear of *not knowing* and potential failure, all such tasks ended up in the pile under her desk. While she walked around carrying "a ball and chain of shame," one she claimed she would do anything to get rid of, clearly, there were some things she could not do. As burdensome as the feelings of shame about the pile were for Sarah, they were, ultimately, more tolerable than confronting the feelings that created the pile.

Once we started to hear from and understand her fear, to give *it* a voice in the dialogue, something it had never been offered, we suddenly had something to interact with other than her inner-parent's judgments. We were in new territory and out of the stale loop of shame and blame. We both acknowledged that it felt as if we had opened a window, and fresh air now filled the room. Without the shaming and blaming that had kept the system stuck and broken— and prevented Sarah from being able to change and heal—there was now room to move, and move she did.

When we feel afraid and overwhelmed in the face of not knowing how to navigate a situation, when anxiety and the need to flee from potential failure arise, rather than avoiding the experience and unleashing a flurry of self-attacks, we need to learn a new response. We need to turn toward our fear, to practice staying with it, feeling our anxiety, and honoring our true experience. Sarah learned to remind herself of the history of her fear, the fact that she had been overwhelmed and unassisted as a child, and that this escapist part of her had good reasons for wanting to escape. Rather than attacking herself for her instinct to avoid (as her inner-parent would have) she learned to comfort herself, to accompany her fear, as one would usher a friend or a child as it walked a frightening path. It was not until she could take her own side, get to know and befriend her real feelings, welcome the original experience that sat under the attacks, that she could start to change and do a better job. Supported by her own kindness, Sarah was finally able to address the pile under her desk and develop the skills that her difficult tasks required.

Not Enough

The fear in this case is that if we are allowed and encouraged to be who we really are, that who we are will not be enough. Our *not-enough-ness* can come in many forms: not enough to be loved, to be safe in the world, to be respected, to be what we are expected to be, to matter, and on and on. Because of this fear, we build a false self, a version of ourselves that we believe will be enough to get us what we need—make us safe in the world. Feeling enough then must continually involve effort and some alteration to who we actually are. The catch, however, is that we cannot gain a true sense of *enough-ness* when that sufficiency is built by and upon a false self.

The antidote to our fear of not being enough is not more self-improvement, more trying, but rather—counter-intuitively—to *stop* trying. Stop trying to be enough, to be a better version of ourselves. In order to feel enough, we must give ourselves permission to meet, and ultimately, be our authentic self, as it is. In so doing, our very sense of *enough*, what it feels like and what it means, begins to transform. We discover that the non-negotiable characteristic of *enough-ness* is that our true self be the one who is living it; we are the mandatory ingredient in the recipe for *enough-ness*. Any sense of *enough-ness* that is generated by way of a false self is useless in healing our fears of inadequacy. Only by showing up in our life as who we truly are, can we genuinely absorb the *enough-ness* that we create. Furthermore, the results that we produce via a manufactured self become not only unusable for self-esteem, but unsatisfying. The external approval we accomplish—by refashioning our truth and repackaging ourselves—ceases to offer contentment or fulfillment. Eventually, "being" and "enough" birth an "is" between them to become: being *is* enough.

Self-Indulgent

In the same family as *lazy* and *stuck* exists our fear of becoming *self-indulgent*. Specifically, our belief is that caring about our own experience will translate into indulging our desires indiscriminately. Rather than lying on the couch doing nothing, we will end up lying on the couch eating bonbons, drinking margaritas, channel surfing (or whatever our most decadent indulgence may be). We will use any kindness towards ourselves as permission to go wild and unleash the out-of-control pleasure-driven animal that we are under our well-behaved façade.

In fact, the opposite is true. People come into my office in a state of craving—constant craving. They are chasing satisfaction and/or relief from a basic state of dissatisfaction, but nothing provides the relief that they crave. If some relief is to be found, it is ephemeral. However, when we are heard correctly, feel truly understood, known, and cared about, we experience an emotional and spiritual nourishment that is deeply satisfying. Consequently, we have less desire to indulge in the pleasures that used to stave off our hunger. When our emotional and spiritual self is truly nourished, through our own care, we end up far less hungry for the things that we used to substitute for *soul* food.

Bad

Religion may be the most powerful thing humans have ever created. Religion, in good hands, can be a profoundly positive force in our life. Religion has the power to connect us with the best of our humanness, to draw us into our hearts, to know ourselves as loved and as love itself. In less good hands, however, religion can be destructive to our sense of self; it has the power to misguide us into believing that our core is bad and that we need something outside ourselves to keep our badness in check. This is religion misused and misinterpreted. In truth, however, religion does not teach us that we are bad; people teach us that we are bad. People mislead us into believing that any kindness toward ourselves will unleash something terrible, namely, ourselves.

Matt was a young man who was raised as a strict Catholic. He was a likeable and charismatic twenty-five-year-old, but it was clear that his range of allowable experience, that which he permitted himself to feel or even acknowledge, was carefully cordoned off like a murder scene. Physical desire, anger, doubt, and even love sat outside the lines of the permissible. Hell fires, disapproving nuns, a rage-filled father, and an angry and judgmental God lurked in every crevice of his imagination. One day as we were taking a walk I asked Matt who he would *be* if he were to follow his basic nature, if the handcuffs were removed and he were able to get up from the pew. The very question alarmed Matt, and just considering it felt sacrilegious. He was not ready for such a direct approach. I had trusted the bond of our relationship, but misjudged the strength of his fear. He dismissed the question with a pat answer, but appeared disconnected and vacant and soon cut our walk short. I worried that he would sever our relationship, but he agreed to a visit for the following week.

The next time we got together, rather than ask him who he would *be* if allowed to be himself, I asked him what he thought he would *feel* if he were allowed to feel what was true for him. His words came with a strength that I didn't expect. "What I would feel? Are you kidding? I think if I allowed myself to feel or . . . God forbid, act on what I really feel I would end up a serial killer, or no, actually I would just spend all day drinking scotch and pleasuring myself in a room full of naked women, and who knows, maybe men too. And then at the end of the day, I would probably go on a killing rampage. I guess with regard to the question you asked last week, this is my basic nature, this is who I would be if the handcuffs were taken off." He described being in high school, when just to have a thought of kissing a girl was absolutely terrifying. It meant that he was a rapist. Why else would he be having such thoughts? It was exhausting for him because he didn't just have to keep himself from committing rape, he had to keep the thought of a girl from appearing, period. He still had not figured out how to make his thoughts stop, which he believed was further proof of the monster he was deep down.

When I asked Matt if he had ever actually thought about raping a girl, he pondered for a moment and then told me that no, he had never had the actual thought, just the fear of the thought. We both stayed quiet for a while, absorbing this truth. Given Matt's beliefs about his basic nature, he was a long way from any kind of faith that his true self could be trusted to lead him anywhere good. Still, we had taken the first step on what would be a long and painful path.

FACING FEAR

Supporting our authentic nature requires us to challenge strong and ingrained fears about who we really are under all our *behaving*. We are steeped in the belief that there is something unacceptable and dangerous about our basic nature. Beneath the rhetoric of positivity, a subtle message exists that it is not wise to support and nurture our true experience, not advisable to stop trying to be a new and improved version of who we actually are. To let ourselves *be* and call off the search to be better, would only invite trouble. Ultimately, we are taught that it is not safe to live by our own truth—not safe to land inside ourselves!

Ironically, we are born undivided, with an instinctive trust in our basic nature. But society teaches us to grow up and out of it, to split into pieces. As we come into contact with the world, we are taught that it is not safe to stay aligned with ourselves, remain as just one entity, united with our experience. We come to believe that we need an internal chaperone in order to be safe, to monitor our intentions and truth. We are misguided into believing that the way to well-being is through the imprisonment of our true self. It is precisely this wrong belief that keeps us separated from ourselves and disconnected from the very source of our in-born well-being.

Well-being requires a willingness to get to know, directly face, and ultimately, walk through our fears, judgments and misunderstandings about our true self. Well-being requires a willingness to support our authenticity, no matter what fear throws in our way— to try on the belief that the fears that tell us that *we* are contradictory to well-being are unfounded and just plain false. Well-being requires a willingness to let go of our old belief that—in order to survive—we need to protect the world and ourselves from who we really are. This belief is precisely that which is making us not okay.

After many years of working with my own monkey mind and heart and the minds and hearts of many others, I have discovered that, contrary to our fears, when we are supported, when our true experience is welcomed and cared for, basic goodness—our true nature—emerges. Put simply, when we receive goodness, we become good.

Conducting fieldwork in the workings of human nature, I have become an eternal optimist on the subject of humans. In the right garden, with the right nourishment and watering, human beings want to grow and move toward the light. More than anything, we all want the opportunity to be good. When asked about our most joyful and nourishing experiences, more often than not we speak of those times when we were able to express our goodness, to help and be kind. When we develop a kind and appreciative relationship with ourselves, we are tilling the garden of our own goodness, creating the foundation for the best of our nature to emerge—enabling ourselves to be the good beings that we are.

4   FEAR OF *WHAT IS*

In the last section we examined our fears about what we will *become* if we dare befriend our own experience. But there exists another set of fears relating to self-kindness: the fears of what will happen *to* us if we treat ourselves with kindness.

Karen is a wonderful mother and friend. Generous in every way, to everyone—but not herself. Karen consistently puts her own needs and desires at the bottom of every To Do list, assuming that her well-being is not as important as everyone else's and that she can do fine without receiving anything for herself. I recently asked Karen what she imagined as the worst thing that could happen to her if she were to take care of her own feelings with the same kindness that she takes care of those of her family and friends.

"If I cared about how I feel?" Karen paused, contemplating this radical idea. "Wow!" she said, "I wouldn't be able to live the life I am living! I certainly would not be able to be in this marriage or do the job I do or, come to think of it, do most of the things that I do."

We are afraid that if we allowed ourselves to experience how we really are, we would have to dismantle everything in our life just to be okay. We are aware that our life is out of alignment, yet we choose to ignore our experience in order to avoid feeling and addressing the *wrongness* and making the necessary changes.

This line of thinking is considered completely logical. We believe that it is better to live a life that is out of balance and fundamentally wrong for us, a life that we have to *check out* of in order to be able to bear, rather than attend to what is real, and possibly give ourselves the option to make it better. Ultimately, the fear that we do not know how to fix our life or that it will be too overwhelming

to try to make changes prevents us from being able to look at the truth of what we are experiencing.

In addition to not knowing how to fix our life, there is a fear of what will happen to us if we allow ourselves to feel our own pain. We are afraid that we will get stuck in the feelings and never come out the other side. The sense is, *If I look at or, G-d forbid, feel my actual life, I will start crying and never stop. I'll never get out alive.* As one client expressed, "It's like I keep all the things that are wrong in my life locked up in my big toe with a big iron gate to seal it off. You are suggesting that I form a relationship with that toe. But if all that stuff gets loose it will completely consume me, and there will be no me left . . . just a big giant poisonous toe."

The first fear, that we won't be able to fix our life if we are honest about how it really is, is a fear whose solution demands a leap of faith. By that I mean, in order to be able to change our life we must first be able to feel it as it is. What we attempt, instead, is to invent solutions to what is wrong, but from outside the experience of *wrongness*, to fix it without feeling it. It is only from inside the experience of our *brokenness* that our healing can emerge. Only the experience itself knows its solution, and not the mind that sits outside it telling us what we need. It is not until we enter *where we are* that we find the imagination and creativity to move to a better place.

I had an experience with my young daughter that exemplifies the way most feelings behave. We were off to a friend's birthday party and suddenly my daughter was struck with a case of the *I don't want to go*-s. The situation escalated quickly into a full-on tantrum within which my daughter decided that the girl who had been her best friend was no longer her friend at all. In fact, this girl was now someone who my daughter despised. Pressed for time, I went the standard route: to convince my daughter that her experience was something other than what it was. *Come on sweetheart, you don't really feel this way; you know you love Lily and you love parties. You are just being silly, now let's go.* But my daughter's feet were firmly planted on the doorstep, her face sullen. I tried again. *You just went ice skating with Lily last week and you had a great time. You will be delighted when you get there, I promise.* Still, no budge, and now her face was turning purple (not usually a good sign). Then suddenly I remembered the book I was writing and decided to befriend the experience that my daughter was actually having.

I took my coat off and moved from standing in front of her with outstretched arms, to sitting down on the step beside her, now joining her physically as well as emotionally. My position change seemed to relax her, and her frown eased. *On second thought,* I offered, *I want to hear all the reasons that you don't like Lily and why you are going to have a dreadful time at the party and why you are so miserable right now. I want to hear all of it and don't you dare leave anything out. If it takes the whole party to get through it, so be it, there will be others!* With a big smile breaking across her face, my daughter happily complied with my request. When she had finished naming her (very short) list of complaints, I made a deal with my daughter that went like this: *We can stay on the doorstep for as long as you want, to see if there are more reasons not to go to the party. Or, we can make a date to meet in the coat closet fifteen minutes into the party and, if every one of your complaints still holds true, we can come home then.* She chose the second option (particularly liking the part about our date in the coat closet). Without saying another word, we put on our coats and left. Fifteen minutes into the party, I found myself alone in a closet with only down parkas for company.

Most feelings, when properly heard and cared for, do shift and heal. Our feelings need a certain kind of attention, one that does not ask them to be anything other than what they are, an attention that is not listening in order to make them change. Our experience needs to be welcome as it is and then, more often than not, it shifts all on its own.

"When am I ever going to get past this anger?" my friend, Peter, blurted out. For years Peter had been carrying around a knot of rage everywhere he went. He was holding on to a disagreement that he had had with a former friend many years ago. What's ironic, however, is that as long as I had known Peter and as long as he had been talking about that same fight, he had never actually been angry. "But that's all I've ever been," he told me, confused and a little irritated when I offered my observation. But had there ever been a time when his anger had really been invited to the table, a time when he was not demanding that his anger be finished? As long as I had known Peter he had been talking about his need to *get on with it*, which applied to everything in his life. He was in a perpetual race to move past whatever experience he was living. I had never heard the anger itself, nor, I suspected, had he. Peter thought for a while and then started to laugh.

In our following conversation, Peter again shared his feelings of humiliation and anger. The words were similar to ones I had heard before, but this time Peter's rage and hurt did the talking. From inside it, he expressed the core of his struggle without demanding that he be done with it or that it be done with him. He did not demand that his feelings resolve themselves, but simply invited his feelings to tea with us, to stay, as if they were our friends.

A month or so later Peter saw the man in question and was surprised by the absence of feeling, the sense of separateness that he experienced from the whole situation. "The whole thing felt like it happened a really long time ago, which it did. This whole thing had more of a *yeah, so what?* quality to it." While Peter was not interested in resuming a close relationship with the former friend, his strong feelings had eased, loosened. They had lost their sharpness, their grip. Peter no longer felt like he had to carry the anger around with him everywhere he went, waiting to punish this man for what he said and did. The anger didn't need him to protect it any longer.

It had had its day. His feelings had been directly experienced and with that the need to preserve them evaporated.

When we befriend our experience without judging or demanding anything from it, our feelings respond by shifting and unknotting themselves. Without a relationship between Peter and his own experience, the knot of anger had remained fixed, as my daughter's feet had remained fixed in that doorway. The kindness and curiosity that we offer our own experience is precisely the healing cure that most painful experiences require in order to shift and move forward.

THE DANGERS OF OUR TRUTH

For some of us, befriending our *selves* is perceived as a threatening venture. Our truth is feared as something potentially destructive to our well-being. When what we feel is not to the liking of those around us—does not make them feel good—we are attacked, rejected, and then blamed for our own rejection. Truth then is synonymous with negative and shameful feelings.

When I first met Samantha, she was certain that were she to express dissatisfaction of any kind, she would be punished and, ultimately, abandoned. Thankfully, I gave her a reason to be dissatisfied soon enough, and Samantha found the courage to tell me that I had made her angry. Rather than verbally insulting her or dismissing her as *difficult* as she had feared and assumed, I expressed my delight in her admission and remarked on her great accomplishment of being honest with herself, and me. Exploring her experience of what I had done to upset her, I came to understand where I had *missed*—where my intention and her experience had gotten so out of alignment. After much dialogue in which I was intent on understanding the experience through Samantha's eyes, ears, and heart, I came to know what Samantha had lived as a result of my earlier comment. I expressed deep regret and sadness that my words had failed to provide the support I intended. I took responsibility for participating in the interaction that had caused her to suffer, for *missing* her as I had.

Samantha did not need to be pathologized for having an experience that was different from what I intended. She needed empathy for the painful experience that she had endured as a result of how she experienced my words. When we are upset by the words or actions of another and are brave enough to tell them of our truth, too often what we receive back is a defense from the other's ego. Our experience is rejected as the other claims their authority. We are criticized and interpreted for our experience, and informed that we should have experienced their words as they meant them, that in some universe of truth/court of law, they were right and we were wrong for having the experience that we had. The fact that our experience did not match the other's intention is viewed as an invalidation of the other's goodness and as a result, our experience must be eradicated.

In the cycle of rupture and repair between Samantha and I, I held her hurt in a container of kindness, acknowledging that her hurt could exist and be worthy of our loving attention, even if I did not intend it. We both heard each other correctly and without judgment. There was no fight for who was right or wrong in the interaction, just an acknowledgment of where we had lost each other along the way and the pain that had been caused. My willingness to move my own ego out of the way, relinquish my *rightness* so that I could know and comfort her experience, was deeply healing for Samantha. Her experience had been more important than my being right. This truth then allowed her to feel genuinely taken care of, and to heal.

The next week I was surprised by what I discovered, and it proved to be a great teaching for me in just how dangerous true experience can feel, even within a container of so-called safety. While I believed that we had created an environment of trust, where her truth could be heard without punishment, I soon understood the fragility of that safety.

Samantha entered the room breathless with the look of a wounded and slightly crazed animal. "You are still talking to me?" she said.

I was confused.

"Come on . . . for last week," she said, appearing unsteadier by the moment.

It was then that she began to weep, crying for several minutes without looking at me. Finally, she raised her eyes. "Do you mean you are not going to tell me that you've had enough of me, that you can't take me anymore, that I am too sensitive, that you can't say anything without my having a problem? You're not going to tell that I am a pain in the ass patient, that you have your own life and don't have time for my constant needs?" She then described her week, how she had been nearly unable to function, certain that she was going to be *fired* by me—convinced that she had lost me. While I had pretended that it was okay to be who she really was, secretly she knew that it was not. Her trust had only lasted as long as she was with me and then her belief that, really, no one could stand her if she were her *self* came back with a vengeance. For Samantha, being who she was translated to certain abandonment—an abandonment that was her own fault, for being someone whose truth was intolerable and burdensome.

It wasn't until Samantha saw my face, the absence of judgment in my expression, my genuine confusion, that maybe, for the first time, she believed that it might be safe to be who she was, and to include her real truth in our relationship. And yet, the instant she shared her vulnerability, expressed her despair over my certain abandonment, a new wave of fear engulfed her. Again, she knew that this truth would be the final straw, the too much, too needy—too *her*—that pushed me away. We were back in the same circle of fear, collapsed into the larger belief that *she* was the very thing that was dangerous.

Over and over, we circled through our dance of fear and recovery as she learned and re-learned that my desire to know her was bigger than anything else, and that I was strong enough to hold her truth and appreciate it in whatever form it came, even if it did not stroke my ego. While Samantha still believed that she was responsible for making me feel good, little by little, she was beginning to trust that making me feel good would not result from offering me a particular truth (one that I liked), but only by sharing the real truth itself.

As time passed Samantha started to build confidence not only in our relationship but also in herself, and what might be possible if she were to allow her true self to exist. "I feel like I keep walking into a mine field and then after crossing it, I realize that I didn't get blown up. Every time I get to the other side, I am amazed. But the more I take the risk, it is as if something fundamental, the ground beneath my feet is shifting. Still, each time I set out into the next minefield, I guess you could say to let my *true self in*, it's equally terrifying. The fear that I will die never lessens."

In order to heal we must be willing to keep venturing into our internal minefields, not knowing if we will get to the other side, but continuing to walk nonetheless. Change requires that we be willing to face the fear of our *self* and, in that face, continue en-*courage*-ing our *self* into our own life, compassionately honoring our intention to know our *self* as is.

GETTING STUCK

While difficult feelings can and do change when treated properly, there are some people for whom any relationship with strong feelings creates a kind of quicksand. Invited into their experience, they end up collapsing into the negative feelings. Once engulfed, no separate, healthy self remains to help them navigate through the feelings and to the other side.

We not only can get stuck in negative feelings, but can create an identity out of them. "Sad" becomes *who we are* rather than something we are experiencing. Because our very existence is then tied up with our sadness, our sad story, letting go of our negative experience becomes ever more challenging. Our sadness is now necessary to the self's survival.

Because we experience sad feelings does not mean that we have to be identified with sadness. There is a fundamental difference between being sad, feeling sad, and being in relationship with sadness. When we are sad, we *are* the feeling and nothing else exists. When we *feel* sad, a separate *I* is present there, an *I* that is doing the feeling. There is someone who is not entirely made of sadness. Furthermore, when we are in relationship with our sad experience, the *I* is even more separate, a presence that can be *with* but not *of* the experience. It is this last presence that is the key component of well-being.

We generally travel through several stages on our way to this kind of presence and often we have to identify with and become our feelings before we can move into a relationship with them. When I first met Marielle, I found it hard to be with her. She was very angry, disconnected from her own feelings and in full agreement with her mother's negative version of who she was. Her relationship with her own experience was critical and impatient. As if trying to pound her despicableness into me, she continually repeated all the things that were wrong with her, attempting to demolish any part of me that might like her. "No one else has a problem with my mother. Obviously I am too sensitive! Why can't I just get over it? What's wrong with me that I need this kind of coddling? My God, I am forty years old and still wanting a mommy who loves me. When am I going to start living my life?"

Marielle was frustrated with her own sadness, for having a response to a mother who could not relate to her feelings. She was exasperated by her own rage, the rage of not being seen or understood by her cold and distant parent. She was disappointed in her own despair, the despair of having a mother who valued only the external world and was never interested in her daughter's internal experience. Marielle was dreadfully ashamed of her own jealousy, the jealousy of her sister's ability to connect with their mother, and of their shared interests. And finally, she was furious at her own rage, the rage she felt at her sister for never having to suffer the isolation and rejection that Marielle lived every day.

Marielle had built a relationship with her own experience that was unkind and punishing. She blamed her experience for being wrong and needy, and shamed it for its suffering: Her loneliness was the reason that she couldn't find the company she craved. Her over-sensitivity was why she could never experience kindness. Her jealousy was why she could never be enjoyed as her sister was. Her need to have a mother that loved her was the reason that her mother could not love her. As she put it, "Who could love someone who needs and demands as much as I do?" Her experience was the cause of its own deprivation. In this scenario, Marielle kept her mother safe, as the good mother, and made herself (and her experience) that which was bad. This relationship with her own feelings kept Marielle imprisoned in a cycle of frustration and pain, mothering her experience as she had been mothered, locking herself inside a life of bitterness and isolation.

As time passed and Marielle learned to trust me, I met the truth that sat beneath Marielle's judgments of herself. I began to hear more from *Marielle's side* and less from her mother's. Together we came to know what it had been like for Marielle to be the daughter of this mother, to have this person as her "caretaker." When Marielle's judgments of herself returned (as they often did), I quickly made her aware of her self-treatment and fiercely refused to join her in blaming herself for her own suffering. I listened to her experience without interpretation or judgment, modeling a new relationship that she could build with her own experience. I took the side of her frustration, grief, and exhaustion, of all the feelings that came from trying to find a path to her mother's heart—and failing. Piece by piece, we carefully unwrapped each of the emotions that lay buried beneath her self-hatred. I bore witness to Marielle's experience and kept company with her isolation. Slowly her blame and shame melted as we both came to know and love the truth that was Marielle's.

With her experience now offered a seat at the table, Marielle moved into the next stage, the (as Tibetan Buddhist teacher, Pema Chödrön described it) "Toys R Us, Feelings R Us" cycle of suffering. Marielle then became more fully identified with her experience, she *was* her painful feelings, inseparable from the isolation, rage, and deprivation she had lived. Marielle now defined herself as someone who had not been loved by her own mother; a person who had been deprived of a basic human right; a person who had suffered. She had found a new identity: she was an "orphan." All difficulty she faced now stemmed from this primary abandonment— of never having been mothered. She had changed sides, aligning herself with her own experience rather than her mother's. This was definitely progress, but we had further to go. While Marielle was no longer trapped in her mother's story about who she was, she was trapped in her own story. No longer a bad daughter, she was a daughter with a bad mother. Her story was based on her own experience and without the painful self-loathing, but still it was a story that limited her full experience of life.

Marielle's mother was still at the center of who she was, and Marielle was still living a life defined by her past—collapsed into and identified with her suffering. While now able to experience the feelings that were under the blame and shame, not enough space had grown between her and her experience for her to be in relationship with her suffering. She had not yet discovered her identity as that presence which could be with her experience, but not inside it, not made of it.

Until this point I had been supporting Marielle in getting to know her experience, to uncover what was true for her. Now I wanted her to know freedom from the prison that her feelings had become, to be released from her identification with the suffering. This had to happen carefully however. She needed to separate from her feelings carefully—separating from but not abandoning them. I encouraged Marielle in developing autonomy, so that the experience she uncovered, the story of her life, did not become fixed as a justification for her suffering, an explanation for why her suffering needed to continue, and why she did not need to take responsibility for creating a new experience for herself.

I was guiding Marielle away from the cause of her pain—from *who* did *what* to her and *why*, and *how* it had ruined her life. My goal was that she experience freedom from her story about her pain so that she could get to know the pain directly. In order to do this, I invited her to bring her body into the dialogue. What did the grief actually feel like as a sensation? Where did the deprivation live in her body? How did the rage present itself physically? With attention to her bodily sensations, her direct physical experience, Marielle could bring definition and form to the emotions that made up her suffering, to shake out the stories that went with the feelings so that we could observe the feelings directly. It was important that Marielle get to know her feelings and sensations in a precise and focused manner, as individual entities that she could investigate. Ultimately, Marielle would be able to relate *with* her feelings rather than to *be* her feelings.

Throughout this process, I was careful to use the impersonal article in referring to the feelings that Marielle was experiencing: *the* feelings not *her* feelings. In order to move forward, Marielle needed to let go of her attachment to *her* sadness, *her* deprivation, the lifetime of unfairness that belonged to *her*—that she believed *was* her. Learning to notice the feelings as physical sensations taking place in particular locations within her body helped loosen the fierce sense of ownership that Marielle held over her experience. By pointing Marielle to the continuous arising and disappearing of emotional contents, the waves of sensation coming and going, I was showing her the independent and ephemeral nature of the experience that felt so fundamentally solid—so inarguably *hers*.

Marielle was learning a new way to relate to her experience, as a separate entity, an *it*. It was a new view of her feelings, as a compilation of independent sensations within a larger container, rather than a generalized state of which she was made. Marielle was a bird of pain, but we were heading into the sky of awareness in which that bird was flying. Her task was to learn to remain wide and infinite, clearly seeing the elements of suffering within her as well as everything else that was there.

As we continued our work together, Marielle's truth, previously an amorphous undefined and inaccessible blob, became a series of distinct physical sensations and expressions. With this more refined awareness, Marielle was able to enter into a relationship with her experience from a number of different perspectives. If she chose, she could enter and indulge in the story of her emotional experience while remaining aware that she was going into the emotional material. Alternatively, she could choose to interact with the experience from a more intellectual standpoint, using her mind to understand why her experience was the way it was, and how it affected her. As well, she could experience her feelings as purely physical sensations, energy dancing, keeping her direct physical experience separate from the narrative that went with it. What was important was that it was now her choice—how she wanted to be in relationship with her own experience. And most importantly, whatever choice she made, she could remain awake to where she was in the relationship with her experience. Marielle was developing a way to be in charge of her own internal state. Where there had been one, there was now two: a Marielle *and* an experience.

As this process moved forward, however, another knot appeared: Marielle had become attached to a definition of herself as an "orphan," to an idea of herself as one who is deprived. In a strange way, she derived pleasure from this new identity. This story about who she was gave her a sense of meaning, existence, and weight; it put her on the map. She was *someone* when defined by this suffering, and Marielle was firmly gripping this version of herself.

With a bit of humor, I brought Marielle's attention to all the different *selves* that she had inhabited throughout our work together, all the versions of who she had been in just the last few years. When I first met Marielle, she *was* a self-described overly sensitive, needy, "pain in the ass," a person who nobody could love. So too, she had gone through a stretch where she was "an empathic, enlightened Jesus Christ, a person who forgave anyone and everyone who had ever hurt her, someone who had transcended pain." There was another *self* that was an angry feminist, whose mission in life was to wake people up to the mistreatment that men had perpetrated on the female animal. As that Marielle, she was someone on whom men had unleashed their crimes, a member of the female tribe. She was made of female suffering. For a time too, she had been a person who would always be alone, a misfit in society, one who was not capable of feeling love in the way that others could, best left to be a hermit. Most recently, Marielle had become a self-identified artist, "a feeling creature and spiritual being" born (sadly) into a family of provincial hacks. Furthermore, it was this true artist self that was the cause of her being unlovable and un-understandable to her family and the world.

These were just a handful of the many Marielles who had walked through my door. Together we enjoyed a chuckle looking back over her colorful parade of selves. Each of these identities had been born out of her own experience, her own pain, and with each came a belief that this was who she fundamentally *was*. Now, as she sat across from me, she was a little girl who had been severed from her umbilical cord of connection and warmth, a flower who had been raised in a fallow field. In her new identity, she was "an abandoned orphan entitled to love."

Marielle began to develop a new presence within herself, an awareness that could notice the identities she had taken on and taken in, all the *I*'s she had inhabited, believing that each contained some fundamental essence of who she was. In the process, she noticed that her *I* was in fact something that she created rather than something that was solid or fixed. Slowly her sense of who she *was* became more aligned with the awareness that could see the identities that she personified, and less so with the identities themselves.

Consequently, the tight grip that Marielle held on her suffering and her most recent version of *self*, began to loosen. Who she *was* was shifting—from a self defined by the contents of yet another story, to a more expansive and eternal presence. Marielle was discovering the essence of well-being: compassionately holding all her different life-stories, while remaining larger than and free from their accompanying identities.

5   WELL-BEING: A RELATIONSHIP WITH OURSELVES

In Chinese philosophy, *Tao* is the word used for the absolute principle underlying the universe. The Tao combines within itself the principles of yin and yang and signifies the *way* or code of behavior that is in harmony with the natural order. It is said that the Tao that can be spoken is not the Tao. The words used to describe this way of behaving are only pointers, leading us to an experience of wholeness and well-being. The same can be said about well-being. All words we use to describe well-being are doomed. The essence of well-being cannot be captured by language. When turned into a concept or idea, it is corrupted and loses its essence; it becomes something other than what it is. Well-being itself can only be experienced and we know it when we are living it.

While we cannot adequately capture well-being with language, we can use words to describe what well-being feels like and what it does not. We can identify some primary ingredients in its fragrance. Webster's dictionary lists well-being as "the state or condition of being in good mental or physical health." Happiness, on the other hand, is defined as "showing or feeling pleasure or contentment." This was a good foundation from which to explore further.

Asking people from all walks of life, I requested a word or two to capture the two experiences. From the field:

Well-being is health, balance, wholeness, peace, alignment, calm, okay-ness, grounded, deep, integrated, good, centered, breathing, still, compassion, not trying, not anxious, what is-ness, strength, thriving, heartiness, robust, potential, lasting, present, being.

Happiness is excitement, pleasure, delight, success, fun, positive, short-lived, sparkle, elusive, elation, energized, pleasing, right now, happening, want, desire, yes, more.

Some preferred analogies. "Happiness is a purple rose. Well-being is an oak tree." "Happiness is a single saxophone's high G. Well-being is the full orchestra's middle C" (from a musician). "Happiness is a raspberry tart. Well-being is the feeling we have after a wonderful meal with good company." "Happiness is chick lit. Well-being is *The Odyssey*." From a mom, "Happiness is my daughter's giggle when she feels the tickle of the toothbrush on her tongue. Well-being is the place in my heart where she resides."

Clearly, well-being is different than happiness. Well-being can exist when we are not happy. It is not dependent upon our current circumstances. It is a presence that sits below the contents of our life, one that can remain steady throughout unstable conditions. Well-being is not transitory or elusive, but rather constant and reliable. It is the eternal now rather than the right now. It is the ocean out of which the waves of happiness and un-happiness arise. Well-being is a way of being as opposed to a way of doing, a state that we feel in our bodies and spirits, not something we know in our heads.

When we are well, we feel calm and unafraid. We can be in a friendly relationship with whatever experience is happening within us, even if it is painful—without the threat of it destroying us. We can face our truth and be curious about our feelings without the fear that they will overtake us. The characteristic peace of well-being comes as a result of not fearing our own internal life.

So too, when we are well, we feel more connected, less separate and alone. The compassionate relationship that we develop with our own experience allows us to feel greater compassion for the experience of others, opening us up to the sense of connectedness that is yet another hallmark of well-being.

Well-being has a depth and a weight to it. It feels grounded and secure. As one friend described, "Well-being keeps your feet on the ground, as if you can weather any storm that comes through." And from another, "It is the feeling I had as a child when my mother would tell me that everything was going to be okay, and I knew it was true." When we are well, there is a sense that all is right with the world even when there is so much that is not right.

TRUTH VS. COMFORT

Well-being provides a different gauge for what a *right* life means. Rather than *whether or not we like it* determining the rightness of our life, well-being trusts *how it is* to be the formula or a *right* life. Well-being requires that truth rather than comfort be our guiding force, our compass. In order to develop a loving relationship with ourselves, we must be willing to acknowledge the experience we are actually having, to honestly face what is, regardless of whether we like or dislike its contents. As Jung said, "We cannot change anything unless we accept it."

If we do not start from where we are and what is true, we are building on a faulty foundation, and thus real change will not take hold. If we are not relating to whom and how we actually are, of what worth is the kindness that we are offering ourselves? To whom or what are we being kind? Kindness is lost on the untrue. Well-being requires us to replace the desire to be comfortable with the desire to shine the light on that which is real. And ultimately, with enough practice, the nature of comfort itself changes. All that is false or hidden then becomes the source of what is uncomfortable, and our truth—no matter what it is—becomes the true place of comfort.

For many of us, a time comes when comfort, as a goal in life, starts to lose its allure. As my dear friend put it, "After a lifetime of perfectly shaken martinis and stellar toys, I suppose I am finally bored with comfort." As a life-goal, comfort often leaves us feeling empty and unsatisfied. We are not uncomfortable, but we are not really comfortable either, not in a deeper sense. Often at the point in life when we have less time ahead of us than behind, a craving arises to feel the burn of the truth. We realize that we don't just want to get through life unscathed, stay safe in our cocoon, but rather want to live life in its rugged realness, with the truth as our ultimate interest. Again in my friend's words, "If the truth is discomfort, then bring it on. At least the truth feels alive, and feeling alive is a goal worth pursuing." Ultimately, the truth can provide a deeper sense of comfort and possibility than anything pleasure can provide.

MAKING THE CHOICE

Well-being requires choice. Not only must we choose to look at our life truthfully, but we must choose to truthfully look at ourselves and our own mind. Well-being can only arise when we agree to take off the costumes that we wear on the inside—to squarely face the parts of ourselves that we hide even from ourselves. Who is it that we are unwilling to show—to ourselves? This is the question that we must choose to examine.

With the help of a few good friends, I was recently able to meet a part of myself that I had, for many years, managed to hide from my own awareness. I write a blog about technology and consciousness for a national site and on several occasions, friends have commented that I sound angry in my writing, like someone who is exasperated and pessimistic about the human race and what technology is doing to it. I have vehemently defended myself, claiming over and over again that I was not angry, but rather afraid—that fear and a sense of urgency were what inspired my vehement tone. I was adamant about convincing my friends that it was in fact my love for and belief in humanity that caused me to speak out so strongly, to try and protect humanity from what I see happening with regard to technology and consciousness. "It is not anger at people but love for people that inspires me," I kept hearing myself say.

And so I started investigating my own insistence, why it was so important to me that I convince others and myself of my not-angry-ness and of my deep respect and love for people. What I found as I peered past my own internal mask was that, while I am indeed terrified by our ever-increasing capacity and desire to distract ourselves with our devices, to be anywhere but here, I am also furious. "Wow, I am furious," I said to my dog who was sitting at my feet, and then I promptly burst into giggles. All this defending of my love for all, and there it was, a ferocious anger at each and every person I have ever seen shouting into their Smartphone on the treadmill, blathering on about the fantastic new app that has changed their life, frantically playing *Angry Birds*, laughing as they scribble scrabble with their online friends, and texting every last bit of minutia that they are thinking . . . you get the point. Furthermore, there are many days when I do not feel hopeful that we, the human race, will make the choice to be present and conscious rather than distracted and unconsciousness. I found out that I had been hiding my own anger from myself. It was only by choosing to investigate my adamancy—that I was not the angry, pessimistic person whom I had unconsciously deemed unacceptable, that I was able to see my own mind more clearly.

So why is it a good thing to discover the unwelcome parts of ourselves? How does it help me to know that I am also angry? There is a reason that I burst into laughter when I realized that I had been hiding my anger from myself. When we acknowledge and accept the parts of ourselves that have been denied, the whole system lightens; our energy is freed up from having to keep the feelings out of sight. As a result, no matter what sort they are, the feelings lose their power. They're there but they don't hold us hostage any longer. We are free to act, and to choose our actions differently if needed. We can stop resisting, fighting against the truth of who we are, and just let ourselves be.

A RELATIONSHIP WITH OURSELVES

Thus far I have been describing what well-being feels like, and some of what it entails, but how do those who have reached a state of well-being behave? What do they know or do that is different from what un-well people know or do? How do we become well if not through the same methods that we have been taught to become happy? If perfecting ourselves and our life situation, or at least our response to it, is not the secret to well-being, then what is?

As mentioned earlier, most people define self-care with a list of external actions—going to the gym, taking more walks, eating out for lunch, getting a massage, using their vacation days, and so on. The concept of what it means to take care of ourselves is external. Self-care has been kidnapped from the internal world and come to suggest something that we *do* to make ourselves feel good. While all of the positive actions mentioned have the potential to improve our mood, they offer only a temporary relief from life's challenges, a short-lived state of pleasure. There is a more profound kind of self-care however, one that is not about muscling through life, but rather a self-care that comes from building a new relationship with our real experience. The kind of self-care that creates well-being is not about changing our external behavior, but about being with ourselves in a new and different way, not just when we remember to steal a moment away from our desks, but all the time.

The relationship with our own experience that leads to well-being is defined by kindness, curiosity, and acceptance. In order to develop well-being, we must build a place inside ourselves that is like a good internal parent, one that can be loving, gentle, and interested in our thoughts and feelings while still remaining larger and wiser than what we are thinking and feeling. When a good parent comforts a child who is upset, he/she empathizes with the child's pain, comforts him, while also knowing (from a more mature place) that his pain will pass and that he will be, and in fact is, already okay. It is the parent's job to remind and reconnect the child with his fundamental okay-ness, that okay-ness which no situation can destroy. The nature of our relationship with our own experience must be of this cloth: supreme kindness within the larger container of wisdom.

In order to create well-being, we must develop an inner presence that is always with us and on our side. This is a presence to whom we do not have to prove that our experience is deserving of care and kindness. This inner-parent holds the assumption that what we experience is important simply because it is so. The inner presence that leads to well-being is interested in how *we* are in the middle of the life we are living; it is *us* and not the situation that is of value.

As well, this inner presence explores our feelings without demanding that they change. It wants to know who we are and how we are, and not a new and improved, *better* version of ourselves. Furthermore, this presence keeps its focus on our intention. Kindness for our feelings is not dependent upon the external success or failure of our efforts. Instead, this inner-parent is aligned with our experience and whether we receive what we were intending to create.

The inner presence that leads to well-being is there to comfort our experience as it is, while simultaneously encouraging us to continue growing. When we start treating ourselves as someone we love, our path through life becomes clearer and more joyful. *We* are included in the journey and as a result, we have our own presence and support to accompany us. Self-kindness is the act of compassionately welcoming our true experience—ourselves—into our own life. With well-being as our new intention and a new code of behavior for our relationship with our own experience in place, we can start practicing this self-kindness, and ultimately, becoming the *I* who will engage in this new relationship.

PART TWO:

BEYOND WELL-BEING

6   *UN-STICKING* FROM OURSELVES

The time has come for us to stop striving for happiness and start realizing our natural state of well-being. Well-being is a state that we can maintain; it is reliable and possible, the result of a specific kind of relationship that we build with our own experience. Thus far, I have been focusing on the first half of that premise, specifically, *the kind of relationship* that we create with ourselves—what that relationship looks like and how to develop it. From here on, I will be looking at the second part of that premise, the *with our own experience* part, and all that such a phrase implies.

To suggest a relationship *with* our own experience implies that there must be two separate entities, an *I* and an experience. Consequently, there must be a self that is not made of our experience. In order for well-being to take root we must *un-stick* ourselves from our experience. A space must grow between who we are and what we are experiencing. Our point of reference, where we are looking at the world *from*, must then shift. Well-being requires that we become separate enough to be an *I* that can be in relationship with our own experience.

Thus far, we have been considering who we are, our *I*, to be synonymous with our experience, but this is not the full story. It is time to try on something different, not contrary, but more expansive. Namely, that we are much larger than just our experience, larger than our truth. In order for well-being to take root, *who* we consider ourselves to be must expand wider than even our own authentic experience. It sounds strange—to be larger than just our experience—and yet there is indeed something larger to realize—a space that includes our experience but is not limited to it. The practice of well-being is not in disconnecting from our experience of life, but rather in shifting our sense of who we actually are. Well-being, at its core, is about discovering a different *I*.

THE FIELD OF AWARENESS

So what exactly is this thing called experience, this thing that we include but are larger than? For the purposes of this book, I use "experience" to mean thought, emotion, and physical sensation—essentially, the whole human story, all phenomena. Experience is everything that is moving through the field of our consciousness, the *stuff* of life.

The question then arises, how can we be something larger than the whole human story? Doesn't the word "whole" imply that there is nothing else? It would seem that way, and yet, paradoxically, the essence of well-being is not in the *stuff* that is moving through our awareness. Rather, it lies in the *field* in which that *stuff* is appearing—the field of awareness to and in which our experience is arising.

Well-being blooms when our identity is no longer determined by the contents of what we think and feel, in the realization that who we are *is* that awareness to which the contents that we used to call *me, appears*. We are not what our monkey mind generates, but the larger awareness that brings it into consciousness. Well-being shows up when we wake up to this truth. And indeed, we can think without defining ourselves by our thoughts, feel without becoming our feelings, and sense fully without identifying with our sensations. We are well when we can live the full contents of our life without becoming any of it. In well-being, we take a step back to witness our experience more clearly, and as we do, our identity comes along with us.

While this may seem complicated or like a lot of work, the good news is that this larger *awareness* is not something that needs to be or even can be created by us, no matter how much work we put into it. In truth it already *is* and needs only one thing—for us to stop trying to create it, stop trying period. We don't need to become it, we *are* it. While counter-intuitive perhaps, the path to well-being requires less, not more.

SURRENDERING TO WHAT IS

For years I read spiritual books that said that I had everything I needed to find peace of mind, that there was no work to be done, that if I longed for peace I needed to stop doing and just be. I thought I was just being, but apparently not, as I was definitely not peaceful. Frankly, I didn't know what all that meant, and "stopping doing" sounded a little too close to "dead" for my liking.

I still hoped that there was a way to *do* being, because that was something I knew I could be good at. I was a type A+ New Yorker who had achieved everything I wanted by figuring it out and working hard for it. The *go out and get it* system had made me a success. Why wouldn't it work for me in finding peace? I was going to be the first woman to figure out and forge the path to peace. And so I gave it everything I had, the real college try. And still, no peace. But like a good type A, I wasn't going down easily. I pushed harder, thought harder, strived harder, meditated harder, sought harder, you name it, I did it harder. And still, nothing. Finally I figured it out—not peace, but that I could not figure it out. I could not get there with my usual tools, in the familiar way. So, too, some part of me also knew that I could not get there until what I was calling *there* was *here*.

My mind could not lead me to peace, this was clear. It was simply the wrong vehicle, like trying to drive a toothbrush. While defeated, my mind was also relieved. There was no level to which my mind could raise itself that would achieve this goal. It simply was not *do*-able. At last my mind could rest. I held up a white flag to the heavens. *I don't know*, I said. *I know I can't know, at least not from the I that has been looking—the I that* I *have known myself to be.* I surrendered, and this was my first step on the journey into peace.

Well-being, like peace, can only be found in this surrender. In addition, well-being, like peace, comes not from figuring out how to possess it, but in changing our sense of *who* it is that is being it. The mind cannot achieve well-being for us; it is another *us* who plays in the field of well-being. When we *un-stick* ourselves from thought, emotion, and physical sensation, we become the *I* that is well—that plays in well-being. The place where we land when we are no longer collapsed and intertwined (or stuck!) in the ever-changing contents of our mind, is the place of well-being

UN-STICKING FROM THOUGHT

Most of us are prisoners, held hostage by our thoughts. Our thoughts drag us around through our days, a bone caught in a dog's mouth. Whatever thought appears, we feel we have to entertain it, solve its problem, engage with its story. While we may feel anything but sleepy as a result of our thoughts, in fact, our true self is anesthetized and covered over by the unceasing blanket of thoughts. We are so unaware as to not even notice that thoughts are ruling our world—constantly arising and constantly being responded to. In this system, we *are* our thoughts; there is no space between us and them, no separate self or awareness to notice the thoughts and their demands for attention. Thoughts enter our consciousness with a honey glaze or maybe more aptly, a *crazy glue* coating. As a result, our identity gets stuck to them. It is not until we wake up, minutes, hours, days, years, lifetimes later, that we realize that we have been gone, absent from our life, stuck inside a prison of thought.

Ironically, the majority of what comprises our thoughts is information we already know. Our thoughts chatter on without breaks, repetitively, saying little of interest and never allowing for silence or for anything interesting to happen. Mostly, our thoughts remind us of what can go wrong, what we are doing wrong, what others are doing wrong, what we need to fear, and what we need to remember that we have not forgotten since the last time we were reminded just a moment ago. Sometimes thoughts remind us of good things too, as in why we should trust ourselves, who loves us, and so on. But most of our thoughts are like background static, noise without any real value, a buzz of grocery lists and repetitive worries about past and future events, an unrelenting river of mostly useless data. We are trying to feel well while simultaneously conducting a constant dialogue with a dreadful radio station dialed up to volume 11 inside our heads.

Creating space from our thoughts means building an *I* that is not obliged to engage with every thought that appears, an *I* that can choose how it wants to direct its attention. No matter how our thoughts beckon us to get involved, convince us of their utmost importance, that we will die if we let one pass, we need an *I* that is *un-stuck* and thus free to choose whether or not to engage in our mind's offerings.

The fact that a thought appears in us does not mean that we have to spend the next hour, day, or week, entangled with it, lost in its contents, our life held hostage by it. When we loosen our attachment to our thoughts, and are less convinced that our thoughts are who we *are*, we are free to become the true driver of our life. The placement of our attention—how and where we live—is finally ours to decide.

As we create space between our *I* and our thoughts, we are able to notice the particular characteristics of our thoughts: what they say, what they assume, what tone they use, what their habits and favorite subjects are, and so on. Separating the *I* that is looking at our thoughts from the contents of those thoughts allows us to slow down the assembly line that is continually passing through our mind. As a result, we are given the chance to actually examine the product that our mind is producing, and most importantly, decide if we want to partake in it.

Loch Kelly, founder of the Natural Wakefulness Center, offers the following: "I wonder what thought I am going to have next?"[3] From this perspective, we can watch our own mind with curiosity, even humor, noticing its particular fixations, tricks, hobbies, as well as the *gifts* it sends our way. When we are curious, we notice that the majority of our thoughts are not new, not important, not interesting, not helpful, or any one of an infinite number of *nots*. As a friend pondered, "Why do I keep telling myself things I already know?" Her question begged an important follow-up question, namely, "If you are telling yourself things that you already know, who is it that you are telling?"

Our mind is like an out of order circuitry system. Out of order, but still firing. The master board throws out material randomly, habitually, but without a gauge for importance, or a sense of discipline. Getting unstuck from our thoughts means building a self that can choose amongst the noise that the system spews out. Once released from the compulsion to engage with each thought that arises, we are free to select from the offerings, to decide if there is anything important or interesting happening inside our head. If not, we are free to be—*in* our life, fully present, living a life that we choose.

Where our attention is, is where we are residing. Where is our attention at this moment? Where are we placing the nectar of our awareness? We are not free to truly create our life until we can notice and determine the movements of our own attention. Indeed, we have the skill to choose how we engage our attention. When we can separate the thought that our mind is generating from the self to whom it is appearing, a new *I* gains authority, the *I* of awareness. This new *I* is then free to direct our attention, and thus, direct our life.

THE POWER OF PRACTICE

So how do we get space from our thoughts? How do we *un-stick* and become this larger *I* that can choose its own direction? Simply put, we practice. We start paying attention to our thoughts, turning our ear inward, listening in to the material that our own mind generates. In so doing, we build a new ground inside ourselves—one that is not made of thought, but can notice thought as it appears before us. As we practice watching the tickertape that continually runs in our head, a new self grows, one that can see the ever-moving contents of our own mind from a place that is still, hear the incessant chatter from a place that is quiet.

We learn a lot of skills growing up, but, amazingly, not the most important one. We are not encouraged to study and know our own mind—to be aware of what is going on in our own premises. Being able to master our own mind is the skill that gives us control of our life, and ultimately, freedom. The more we practice paying attention to our thoughts, the better we get at it. In the process, our awareness grows stronger. Our gym for this practice is life. We are building the muscle of awareness, and it is this particular muscle that allows us to *un-stick who* we are from the conversation our mind generates, to liberate our identity from the contents of our thoughts.

Stephanie was a stay-at-home mom of three when we started building her awareness muscle and, in the process, uncovering her true *self*. Stephanie's mind was filled with lists, duties, and endless chatter about the responsibilities that needed her attention. Early in our work, I asked if she could make a list of all the things she needed to remember, just for that particular day. She laughed and said that it would be impossible. Nonetheless, she agreed to try, asking if I had at least a ream of paper and a bucket of pens.

When all was said and done, the day's list contained thirteen items to remember: pick up her daughter Lily from school, drop off her eight-year-old's soccer cleats, buy a birthday present for a friend, schedule a meeting with the English teacher, make Christmas vacation reservations... I'm only five in and my guess is that you're already bored. Now imagine listening to that list all day every day, and that's actually how we live! Stephanie and I had all the day's responsibilities down on just one small piece of paper, and she was clear about what needed to be done to accomplish each task. As she put it, "For a woman with two masters degrees, none of this is rocket science."

Theoretically, Stephanie (or Stephanie's mind) could now stop babbling. No more reminders, clarifications, or conversations were needed; she could move on. I suggested that she check her list two or three times during the day, just to be sure that she was remembering everything, but when not checking, she release herself from having to pay attention to the chatter that was filling her ears. Stephanie had permission to take a vacation from her mind. We were in agreement; there was nothing in the onslaught of thoughts that still needed her attention.

While on vacation from her repetitive, task-oriented thoughts, Stephanie agreed to notice if any new thoughts appeared, maybe something that she actually *wanted* to think about, something that genuinely interested her. I suggested that she pay attention to whether anything surprising made it through to her attention. Would there be a moment of curiosity in her day? In addition, I asked if she could notice how her mind adjusted to this exercise. Did the act of being specific about her tasks make a difference? Did her thoughts quiet? Get more aggressive? Did her mind simply continue to spew out thoughts about her already-known duties, perhaps adding my assignment to its list, poking her all day with false reminders, prohibiting the holiday that I had prescribed?

In addition, I asked Stephanie to watch for how she attended to her thoughts when they arose. Did she begin executing the task that her thought was reminding her of, or making a plan to do so, thereby creating a potential *check mark* beside the thought? Or, did her thoughts remain like toys strewn about a cluttered floor, as she frantically danced around the room, fretting? Finally, I asked Stephanie if she could notice how her thoughts appeared—in what form? Did they swirl like a tornado, un-defined, gas-like? Did they blend into one continuous, background, white noise, a dull static?

Did her thoughts appear individually like random sparks, flashes on a screen? I wanted her to start to pay attention not only to the thoughts themselves, but also to the style in which they presented. I gave Stephanie a number of different ways to pay attention to her thoughts—the who, what, where, and when of them—as I did not yet know which style of observation would be most natural for the new separate-from-thought self that we were building.

When Stephanie returned the following week, I asked what it had been like for her.

"What was *what* like?" she asked.

"Our exercise—taking a vacation from having to respond to your thoughts."

"Oh my gosh," she exclaimed, blushing. "I completely forgot to think about my thoughts. Wow! I really wanted to. That sounded like such an interesting idea."

She had left my office fully intending to and interested in investigating her own mind. Her mind, however, had other plans, and was obviously not as interested in my assignment nor in becoming our guinea pig. Swept up in a bevy of thoughts before she could even begin to pay attention to her thoughts, she had not noticed that she had not noticed. We both laughed. We were not there to judge her mind, or her, but rather to attend to precisely the event that had occurred when she left my office, and the mind that created it. It was a good starting point and evidence that we were on the right track. Stephanie, like all of us, simply needed to practice this new skill.

Over the following year, we continued to return to the exercise of that first day, and, with practice, Stephanie became more aware of her mind's machinations and more skilled at noticing the specific thoughts that her mind was projecting onto her inner movie screen, even gaining a sense of humor about the "sheer boringness" of her own material. As she later described, "On a good day, it is as if I am sharing my internal world with five five-year-old boys, the ADHD sort, who have just eaten a bucket of fudge. The five-year-olds are in one room, a padded cell, luckily, and I am in the room next door. My room is comfortable, like one of those ante rooms you wait for a massage in, with southwestern flute music playing softly. I can hear the boys screaming and dancing and raising the roof, just doing their five-year-old thing. But I know they are safe and do not need me to do anything for them. I know too, that if there is a real emergency, they will get my attention. Until that time, what they are saying is really not that interesting! I have the freedom to do my thing without having to attend to them. They are wild and fragmented and that is just what they are, they don't need and in fact cannot be tamed. I can attend to this quiet space without worry, and what a relief that is."

Stephanie was learning that the mind's basic state is agitation. Its resting place—restlessness. It needs something to ruminate over, to address, to fix, in short, to do. The mind only feels alive when in motion. The mind does not *be*, it does. Well-being does not require us to correct the mind's wild, impatient, agitated, restless nature any more than we would try to correct a golden retriever puppy from being puppy-like, or a five-year-old from being five. Rather, well-being is about finding a way to get comfortable with the mind's agitated nature, to develop a non-restless place inside that can be with the restlessness, allowing the mind to be the mind without having to control it or be controlled by it. The mind needs to want; we can let it want without feeling that we need to provide. The mind needs to do; we can let it do without feeling that we need to do anything about it.

THE FEAR THAT FIGHTS AWARENESS

As we *un-stick* from thought, fear appears. Fear is a powerful opponent for awareness, skillful and accomplished at tucking us back in bed, and back to sleep. When we start to look at our thoughts, we are essentially telling the mind that we are not it and the thoughts it

Noticing that we have been trapped in thought is something to celebrate. We were awake enough to notice that we were sleeping! Our real self is showing up and getting stronger.

Are You Still Awake?

As delightful and confidence building as our growing awareness is, we cannot get too comfortable within it. Remember, we can and will use thought to construct a story or make an identity out of being someone who is a *good* meditator just as we can and will out of being someone who is a *bad* meditator . The story might go something like this:

> *Wow, I am really good at this un-sticking thing, I am a really good meditator, maybe I'm already enlightened. I get it, I really am not my thoughts. This is cool, I have to tell people about this. Now that I have this thing down, maybe I'll go to India and become a yogi, or a guru. This is so easy for me I wonder why everyone says this is hard, I can do most things really well, I wish I would be recognized for all I can do . . .*

When we like the contents of our thoughts we are often more inclined to want to identify with them, to lose our perspective and thus stop examining our thoughts. We are easily seduced and anesthetized by what the mind tells us about ourselves. When our thoughts are about our identity, it is trickier to keep our awareness tuned in. And yet, a positive idea of ourselves is just another bundle of thoughts. This is not to say that we cannot agree with our positive thoughts about ourselves, we can and we should. But it is important to remain aware of such thoughts, to notice what the mind is thinking and saying to us about *us,* just as much as we notice what it is thinking and saying to us about everyone and everything else.

We must keep the muscle of awareness limber and strong so that it is able to maintain itself even in its own playing field.

∾

While I have described only a few examples of thought patterns that have the potential to put us back to sleep when we are *unsticking* from thought, there are infinite varieties of such thoughts, infinite forms in which thoughts related to our growing awareness can appear hidden in the guise of *truth*. Our particular psychology dictates the costumes in which our thoughts masquerade. Wherever we are, thought is, and rarely with flashing lights announcing itself as thought. The larger and stronger our awareness, the better we are at recognizing thought in its different disguises, and the more able we are to maintain our awareness without getting seduced back into the mind's lair.

Choosing to watch our monkey mind with curious and compassionate eyes (and hopefully a bit of humor) offers us some distance from that mind. Who is it, after all, that is watching this mind? As we acknowledge our particular mind's propensities and qualities, we are simultaneously identifying with *that*, the awareness that is doing the acknowledging. While our mind has both lovely and not lovely characteristics, simply by looking at it honestly, and without judgment or expectation, we step into a new identity—not the mind, but rather the source of kindness, which can unconditionally welcome this lovely and not lovely monkey into the whole being.

UN-STICKING FROM SENSATION

When we are in pain, we are in pain. When we are feeling sick, we are sick. Our physical sensations swallow our identity. We become whatever we are feeling. Un-sticking from our thoughts about what is happening in our body means being able to become aware of the physical sensations that are arising within us, but without the stories that go with the sensations. In other words, to be able to notice what is happening in the body from an I that is not collapsed into the sensation itself. I am in pain becomes I am experiencing a sharp sensation in my knee. I am sick becomes I am feeling a queasy sensation in my stomach. We develop an awareness that can maintain itself even in the face of pain and physical discomfort, an I that can notice physical sensation in all its particularities, but without getting swallowed up in it.

The sensation of physical pain, while challenging to live with, is not what is dangerous to our identity. Instead, it is the thoughts and feelings that go with the pain that are the quicksand for our sense of self, the thieves of our attention. De-identifying from physical sensation relies on our ability to refrain from collapsing into the thoughts and emotions—the stories—that our pain triggers.

What does this sensation mean? Before we can even feel what a sensation feels like, we are barreling down the tracks inside this thought/question, deep into a story (usually catastrophic) about where this sensation will lead us, what it implies, and how it will change/ruin our life. Fear then pulls us deeper into the thoughts and emotions about what is happening in our body. What a moment ago was just a sensation is now an epic story, complete with a role for us in the drama. We are gone, as is our awareness, our separateness, consumed by the thoughts and feelings that accompany fear.

What do I need to do about this sensation? Yet another thought train that kidnaps our attention when negative body sensations arise, this train delivers a particular brand of anxious thoughts, namely, thoughts about the tasks that will need to be completed as a result of this sensation. *Who will need to be consulted? Where will I need to go? How will I manage all this?* are a few of the cabooses attached to this train, but regardless of which one we board, we are departing from our *now*, re-attaching ourselves to thought.

Why is this sensation happening? Highly seductive by nature, this bundle of thoughts tries to make sense out of something that usually doesn't make sense. When our body is in pain, our mind wants to create order, to do away with the unknown, to eliminate fear. It wants to take control of a situation that feels out of control.

When we jump on this train, we collapse into thoughts of explanation, the Why-s? of the pain. Such explanatory thoughts replace any direct experience of the sensation itself, obstructing our ability to stay separate from our thoughts, to live in the moment and what is occurring inside our *now*.

At the same time, the mind's attempt to find a logical explanation for what is happening in our body is not always an impediment to our ability to stay awake in the *now*. Sometimes, making sense of a sensation can actually help us remain aware to our *now*. If we decide that our stomach hurts because the butter was left out too long, we may be able to experience the ache in our stomach with a little more attention and without the fear and the story that might otherwise accompany it. If we think that the pain is not going to kill us, we might even be able to be a little curious about what the sensation in the belly feels like. In this case, thought offers us a separate and safe vantage point from which to observe the body's experience, and thus an opportunity to stay present in our *now* as it naturally unfolds.

*Un-stick*ing from sensation involves learning to experience bodily sensation itself, separate from its cause, its consequence, its meaning, or the actions it will require. ***What does this sensation actually feel like? Where is it felt in my body? How does my body live this sensation?*** These questions can only be asked from a place, an *I*, that is *with* sensation, as it is arising, and not stuck inside the myriad thoughts *about* it. Well-being involves being able to bring our curiosity not just to our thoughts, but also to what our body is living, and ultimately, to be able to stay present with whatever mental or physical sensation is happening on our own premises, right now.

I once heard about a meditation teacher who had a degenerative brain disease. What was remarkable was that he could sit and maintain awareness of his mind even as it physically deteriorated before him. He was able to watch his own mind losing its way, turning in circles and becoming frantic about what was happening to it and to *him*. Many were privileged to experience his process alongside him, to be in company with that awareness which could remain separate not only from his mind's terror but from the body's own degeneration. He was a living example of the presence that is neither mind nor body, but in kind relationship with both. The compassionate *now*.

UN-STICKING FROM DESIRE

In order to realize our new aware self, we must also become separate from and observant of our own desires. Advaita Vedanta (a branch of Hindu philosophy) uses the chariot as a metaphor for human life. Our body is the chariot itself, the horses our senses, the reins our mind, and the charioteer/driver our aware, discerning, higher wisdom or true self. When we are fully identified with our bodily desires, our physical senses, we are no more than a brake-less, broken-wheeled chariot whose driver is asleep even while holding the reins. We careen this way and that, captive to our sensory preferences, our horses, as they lunge toward pleasure and bolt from pain. We are without any control or choice of our destination.

Desire is an entity, a sensation that we experience, ever-changing, ever-present. Desire flashes endlessly inside our bodies and minds. Transitory by nature, our likes and dislikes, our *feel-goods* and *feel-bads* need not enslave us. When we practice noticing our physical and mental desires from a place that is not collapsed inside them, we are re-situating our point of reference from the chariot to the charioteer, evolving from a helpless object attached to the back of a runaway chariot, to a more evolved and purposeful intelligence charting its own course. Holding the reins of the chariot, we can notice the pull of our horses, but we—as driver—are who decides our path. With this expanded vision, we are truly free, controlled by neither mind nor body.

UN-STICKING FROM IDENTITY

Our identity is a giant tapestry of thoughts—so tightly interwoven as to become almost unrecognizable as the thoughts that they are. If we look closely, however, we can see that the labels we use to identify ourselves are just bundles of thoughts stuffed with opinions, preferences, and beliefs, which we then weave together to form a story about who we are. Our *I* is made up of thoughts about who we are, based on still more thoughts about what we believe.

If I say, "I am a Buddhist," where is this *Buddhist-ness* that I claim as me? I cannot find it. Unraveled, "I am a Buddhist" is a thought about who I am based on another set of thoughts with which I agree. "I am a psychotherapist" is a thought about who I am based on a task that I perform, a wisdom that I have gained, a set of skills that I possess, and an intention that I hold. The most controversial perhaps for me to unravel, "I am a mother," is another thought about who I am based on something I do (take care of my daughters), events that took place (giving birth to my children), and something that I feel (love). But as we know, one can identify herself as a mother without any of these being true, without taking care of her child, giving birth, or feeling love. So again, "I am a mother" is a thought about who I am based on how I decide to define myself. In truth, our children would be better off if the right to self-identify as a mother or a parent were limited to those who could perform the actions implied, namely *taking care* of and *loving* their child! But ultimately, all of our identities are just *hats* filled with thoughts that we wear as if they were who we fundamentally are.

So what lies under all our *hats*? Or, put another way, who are we if not the sum total of our accomplishments and activities? One thing is certain, a deep sense of relief comes when we are finally free to toss our hats and stop fighting to be *somebody*, to be more important versions of ourselves. What a relief to not have to defend our accomplishments as if they contained some fairy-dust-essence of who we are. What a relief to get to just be who we are, and not have to constantly show it, prove our worth, defend our opinions as if we were establishing our very existence. From Sela, a client: "When I visit my family now, and they are the way they are: busy talking about themselves, never stopping to ask about me, never bothering to ask what I am up to or anything else, never noticing that I am still there, I can actually relax and just be there without having to prove myself or prove that I exist. It's like I don't have to shove in the information about me that would make me a presence. It seems that this larger *I* that I am building can be there even without having anything material known about me. That 'me' that used to feel enraged and unknown, because nobody knew me, or maybe more aptly, knew anything *about* me, well that me is relaxing. Nothing has changed on the outside, but I don't feel invisible on the inside anymore. Even when naked, without all my hats. I guess you could say that my presence is no longer reliant on that former ego identity being known. For years I butt into the dialogue with stuff about me, what I was doing and accomplishing, what I stood for, but that never made me feel any more known. If anything, it left me feeling more pathetic, desperate, and empty!"

Sela was developing a different sense of who her *me* was, and realizing that in fact no effort was needed for that presence to hold a seat at the table. "I keep looking for that old rage that used to get fired up by their self-involvement, but it just isn't showing up. Oddly, what I am noticing is a slight whiff of compassion for my family, for their having to keep spouting their achievements, proving their importance over and over again, confirming that they matter, solidify their own existence. As if they think that all of that stuff that they believe and know and do is all that they are!"

Sela had discovered something much bigger than any words could display and maybe more importantly, uncovered someone or something that no longer defined itself by the information she would have used to describe herself, if asked.

Kristina offers an example of a different kind of shift that occurs when we let go of our accomplishment-based identity. Kristina was a musical child protégée. She played the saxophone from the time her hands were big enough to hold the instrument and now she was a well-known professional saxophone player in a big band. She also had her own band and wrote original music. "I met someone new and didn't tell him I was a sax player," she said, nearly breathless, referring to her new suitor, Jonathan. "I just forgot. I mean it didn't come up and I never even thought about it. I realized after, that I had never announced it or worked it into the dialogue." Not surprisingly, leaving that information out had made her very anxious, at least at first. She had even thought about calling Jonathan and telling him, in some drummed up way, that she was a sax player, "a real one that people had heard of." But in the end, she had decided against it. "I felt like it might be all right—just as an experiment— to be known as whomever that person was who showed up in the conversation with Jonathan, without the big title of musician to justify or prop me up."

"Can you be known without it?" I asked, curious.

"It feels odd, really odd, and kind of naked. But also free. I get to be whoever I am in that moment. Wow, that's an amazing concept. But there was definitely great anxiety about leaving it at that."

She thought for a minute. "But the anxiety came later. It felt like my ego went crazy; it kept telling me that I had sold myself short, like he wouldn't know how important I was, he wouldn't know me. That's why I thought about calling him back, to make sure he knew that the person he was just speaking with was *somebody,* and that he would take away a correct image of me!"

We both laughed, not *at* her ego, but *with* it and its desperation. In truth, her ego was just trying to adjust to a real shift in Kristina's identity. Who Kristina considered herself to be was no longer just her ego, but rather, something larger that could sustain itself even when stripped of her ego's fancy clothes.

During the actual conversation with Jonathan, Kristina did not need him to hear about her uniqueness or her resume. "Surprisingly, I still felt very *there* in the moment without all that about me being known," she said. "In fact, I felt unencumbered without all that information in the way of me. *I*, whoever *I* is these days, could just relax and be there, responding directly to whatever came up. All that other stuff about my saxophone didn't feel like what was important to know about me. That's it really: that information, while impressive maybe, just felt like that, information about me, and not actually me."

Without the compulsion to describe who she was, Kristina's *naked* self was free to be there, to participate in the conversation. Kristina had allowed Jonathan to actually meet her instead of hear *about* her. Kristina had trusted that she could be known simply by being present in the conversation, by allowing herself to fully enter the experience. She concluded, "In the interaction itself, there was only a *now*, no past, no future, just presence, and that's what I was too. I was *nowness*. How exhilarating! Scary in a way, but wonderfully free."

We land in the present moment when we stop trying to do something with it, trying to use the moment to say something about who we are. When we stop describing, showing who we are, we get to *be* who we are. As a result, we can be truly known. We discover our own true identity when we *un-stick* from all the stories about who we are, the hats that cover us up. Our presence in the now *is* us.

UN-STICKING FROM EMOTION

Emotion is the hardest aspect of experience from which to *un-stick*. We can learn to see our thoughts going by, notice our physical sensations, recognize our desires, and acknowledge our identity hats, but to form a relationship with our own feelings is another tea party full of monkeys! We have been taught that if we feel sad, we are sad. If we feel unworthy, we are unworthy. In order to be in relationship with our own emotions, some identity would have to exist that could be *with* our emotions, feel *for* them, but without being them. Can we relate with our sadness without feeling entirely sad, be *with* our sense of unworthiness from a place that doesn't share the unworthiness? This would imply that some part of us can remain separate from and larger than even our own emotions. You might ask, *If I am not made of my emotions, then what am I made of? How could I possibly not be what I feel? What else is there?* We have been taught to believe that our feelings are fundamental to who we are.

The process of *un-sticking* from our emotions is further complicated by the fact that we are emotionally attached to our feelings. As a friend described, "My feelings contain a piece of my heart." And another, "I feel like my feelings are my children. I guess I love them in a way." Noticing our emotions would mean that we would have to let go of them just a little bit, at least enough to be able to be *with* them. *Being with* our emotions can feel like we are abandoning our children, severing the merger between us and them. And, indeed, this can present a real challenge.

Jane was a wise, conscious woman who had practiced meditation for many years. During our work together, a family situation arose that triggered disturbing memories and feelings from her early childhood. The circumstances brought up the deepest pain in her and took her back, emotionally and physically, to a place where she felt unsafe and unwell. Previously I had witnessed her in relationship with her thoughts, her bodily sensations, her emotions, the majority of her human experience. She would get caught now and again, slipping into identification with her experience, but it was short-lived, and even from within the identification she was aware that she was stuck. But here was a tsunami of emotions. Her awareness of the experience, or even of knowing that she was inside the tsunami, was engulfed.

Jane was suffering, tossing around inside this giant wave of pain. When we tried to find a place within her that could be *with* her pain, the pain would end up sucking her under. There was no safe place from which she could relate *to* her experience, no place where her early childhood pain did not kidnap her identity and along with it, her *now*.

After some trying, Jane became aware that she could not separate from the pain. This awareness was a huge step forward. Some part of her could distinguish that she was trapped, inside the pain, which implied that some part of her was aware enough to be outside it. Ever more encouragingly, Jane became aware that she was not unable, but rather unwilling to set this particular pain even an inch to the side of her. She was not willing to be *with* it, and not *of* it. To be *with* it felt like abandoning her emotions, the deepest of her beloved suffering. To abandon her suffering would be to again leave herself alone in that awful dungeon of childhood. The idea of finding a place within her that was separate from her suffering and did not carry its wound felt almost more excruciating than the pain itself. She was convinced that she would not step outside of it, as there was no place in her that was not of it. How then to be well, to find the place of well-being that could be in kind relationship with this experience, but from inside the pain? This was our challenge.

I started by asking Jane to identify what the emotional pain felt like in her body, to feel it as physical sensation. Before beginning to investigate, however, we first consulted with the part of her that was unwilling to separate from her trauma, asking *it* if this exercise was okay for her to attempt. With *its* permission, we proceeded, carefully, down into her body. As Jane searched her physical premises for the experience, the emotion emerged as something sharp, hot, and swirly. This was the beginning of her suffering becoming an *it*, a *something* that she experienced, as opposed to just *her*. As she got more precise, the physicality of the suffering turned to sharp and searing, "like a hot poker." It occurred in the center of her chest. And with the poker, there was a sensation of weight throughout her torso, bearing down on her like a truck. She labeled the sensation "rage" and then "radical unfairness." We got a sense of what the emotion felt like as a sensation, how it took shape within her. Slowly, we were building a relationship with the emotions that had swallowed her hard-earned awareness.

As the months passed, we unpacked Jane's emotional world, all that was buried in the "radical unfairness," bathing it in our kind and curious attention. Jane and I offered the warmth of our company to her feelings, holding space for them without abandoning them, caring for them without becoming them. As a result, Jane learned that she could relate *to* her emotional experience, as something that was a part of her life story rather than her essence or identity. Most importantly, Jane learned that this part of her deserved compassion. Together, we applied radical compassion where there had existed only radical unfairness. It was this compassion that proved to be Jane's doorway to a new and larger sense of self.

Jane's fear that being separate enough to comfort her pain meant abandoning it, also began to ease through this process. She realized that she could best serve her pain by offering it her kindness and loosening the strangle-hold she held on it (and thus that it held on her). In order to bring true comfort to her suffering, she had to be the larger parent to her wounded child, to be *with* her emotion—not *it*. Jane experienced a deep sense of relief as her emotion absorbed her company rather than her identity.

In truth, we want and need a separate grown up presence that can protect us and lead us out of where we are, even as our pain is screaming for us to stay with it in its terrible place. We need something or someone to sit beside us and not be where we are. Our very young pain lacks the wisdom to know that we do need to leave it just a little bit, to be just to the side of it, in order to actually make it feel better. Our own empathic company is a gift of kindness to ourselves, and not the abandonment that we so believe. This awareness is the more evolved wisdom that both blooms from and gives life to well-being.

THE CORE BELIEFS/ CORE EMOTIONS

The most difficult of all feelings to gain perspective on are core beliefs about ourselves. Core beliefs are complex mixtures of unformulated and unresolved early-life experience, a big soup of feelings and thoughts that get absorbed into the mind and turned into a story about who we are and our place in the world. Often, we are not even aware of these core beliefs and yet they determine everything we do!

Boiled down, Mark's core belief about himself was that he was *wrong*—that there was something inherently broken and not right about his being. He had a mother who was highly critical of him, and a father who blamed him for everything that had ever gone wrong. Mark remembered wondering as a young child why his mother did not love him, still believing at that early age that he was a pretty good kid. "I was cute, smart, funny, and always kind, but that didn't seem to be enough. Whatever it was she might have liked, I didn't have it."

Slowly, the assumption that he was a good kid withered, and in its place formed a core belief that there was something fundamentally wrong with him that made him unlovable. He spent the next thirty years trying to figure out and correct whatever it was that made it impossible for his mother to enjoy him. With each new situation or person he encountered, he would immediately decide the cause of the rejection that was heading his way. He was too unattractive, too uncoordinated, too dumb, too provincial—I had heard them all. These self-rejections arrived long before he gave himself the chance to be known. No new experience, skill, accomplishment, or reassurance could shake Mark's core belief that he was, at his core, irreversibly unlovable.

Mark was an example of someone who was fully identified with his core belief. Furthermore, he was without any awareness of the presence of this belief. His core belief sat behind his vision and version of the world. It was his reality. I focused first on offering Mark an experience of himself that was radically different than the one he had experienced with his parents and, indeed, himself. I treated him as the lovable person that he was, perfect in his uniqueness, delightful. I aligned myself with his feelings, relentlessly taking his side and providing the support and empathy that his parents had failed to offer. My hope was that Mark would have an experience of himself as deserving of the love and kindness that I was offering, that he would be able to re-inhabit that perfect child who had been stuck in a childhood that was unfair and undeserved. My aim was to help him feel the tragedy of his perfection having been *missed* by his caretakers, the heartbreak of his having been the son of parents who could not celebrate him as their child. I wanted Mark's heart to break for his own experience. With a different experience of himself, and a growing awareness of what he had taken to be the *truth* about himself, I was hopeful that we could begin investigating the core belief that had shaped his life. And ultimately, I was hopeful that Mark's core feelings about himself could then shift into something more loving and self-supportive.

Unfortunately, offering loving kindness to someone whose core belief is that they are undeserving of loving kindness is often the wrong tact—a futile venture. Mark's core belief about himself sat beneath everything that he experienced, including kindness. His unlovable self-sensor blocked any kindness or love from getting through. Any feeling that was contrary to his core belief was rejected as misguided or invalid, and thus useless in creating change.

As Mark perceived it, I was not only wrong about him being delightful, but now untrustworthy for wanting to give him anything other than what he deserved, namely, rejection. Despite my offering Mark a different external experience, I was failing to provide him with a different internal experience of himself. He and I could not love his *un-lovable-ness* into *loveable-ness*. Since I could not connect Mark with the unfairness of his having been rejected by those who were supposed to love him, I decided to change gears and simply name the enemy.

"You hold a belief that there is something irrevocably wrong with you, in your core, and as a result, that you are unlovable." I said—gently. "Because you believe in this basic flaw in your being, you also believe yourself to be the cause of your own suffering. In truth, you have taken both your mother and your father and swallowed them into your core—your experience of yourself has not moved from the way you felt about yourself in their company. You are living in the family living room all these years later."

It doesn't usually happen so quickly, but this turned out to be Mark's ah-ha moment. In an instant, Mark caught sight of the eyes through which he had been seeing himself, and the world. Naming Mark's core belief of *wrongness* turned out to be the TNT that blasted him out of his old identity box. Putting a frame around his belief shook free a larger identity in Mark, a presence that could see the belief that he had taken as truth, the belief that had ruled, and destroyed his life.

Becoming aware of a primary belief, inviting it out into the light, serves to wedge a space between us and *it,* thereby *un-stick*ing the two. In so doing, it becomes possible to investigate the assumptions that cloud our vision as we interact with the world. We build a larger set of eyes, a new reference point, and consequently, a new self. With core feelings shaken out from our *I,* we are liberated from the prison of distortion that core beliefs create, and thus set free to see *what is* more clearly. The feelings which, for Mark, had felt like the solid nucleus of his being, once illuminated, could no longer sustain themselves, and thus began to unravel and disintegrate, powerfully demonstrating their intrinsically mutable and ephemeral nature.

∾

In order to discover well-being, we must build a relationship of kindness with our own experience. We can only build this relationship if we can relate *to* and *with* our experience, can be connected to, but not merged with it. We discover well-being when we liberate our identity from the prison of mind, from the contents of our thoughts, feelings and sensations. We uncover well-being when we shift our allegiance from our experience to the awareness which brings that experience into being. *Un-stuck* from the movements of mind, we find—and become—the larger space in which well-being resides, the presence from which well-being is derived.

7 STAYING HERE *NOW*

In order to stay separate *from* and still in relationship *with* our experience, we must be able to stay *in* the present moment, as experience comes and goes through our *now*. Our awareness must stay tethered to this moment even as our thoughts, feelings, and sensations beckon us to depart with them on a train to the past or future. Being able to stay in the now is our strongest defense against ending up back in the mind's prison, on the roller coaster of happiness and suffering. Once we have left the now, we have lost our ability to be in relationship with our experience, and with it, our larger self. This larger self can only live in the now; it is *now-ness*.

STAY IN THE BODY—THE ANCHOR OF AWARENESS

We need an assortment of practices, a well-being toolbox, to keep our selves here, tethered to this moment. The force of gravity keeps us physically grounded on the earth without our having to do anything to make that happen. But unfortunately, our presence does not respond to the earth's gravitational pull. However, our physical presence, our body, is the anchor for our present awareness. The body, paid attention to, is what keeps us in the *now*. Bringing our awareness down from the mind into the body, grounding into our own felt presence, directly experiencing what this moment feels like in the body—these are the methods that keep us tethered to the present. The body, directly experienced, instantly creates space from the feelings that threaten to swallow us, the thoughts that beg to distract us, and all the mental movements that steal us from here.

Pamela was submerged in emotion when she arrived at my office. Her physical body had shown up, but she—her presence—had disappeared into the past and into her pain. She sighed heavily; "I am overwhelmed." Then she proceeded to tell me a story about what her husband had said as she was on her way to a recent doctor's appointment. "I hope the doctor doesn't tell you something big and bad and send you for lots of testing," were his words. For two days now Pamela had been furious at her husband, and everyone else in her life. She had lost her emotional footing and was unable to free herself from the pain that this comment had triggered. "Did he really think that would be a helpful or comforting thing to say? I mean, is that really what he thinks would help me?"

Pamela could not remember a time when she had felt comforted or taken care of by anyone. While highly productive and competent, a deep anxiety had always been the wallpaper for Pamela's emotional world, manifesting most often in a terror of illness. And now she was not feeling physically well. She had felt bad for months. It was a scary time.

Her husband's comment had re-triggered intense childhood feelings of being unknown and neglected emotionally. "Who would say that to someone who is already starting from a place of doom? How could someone who knows me say this to me? *This* was his version of taking care of me in that moment of fear. And this is the caretaker I chose!"

In her head, Pamela knew that her husband loved her, that he did not intend to hurt her, that his attempts to soothe her were well intentioned. But his words were unrelated to what her heart needed, out of touch with her actual needs. She had so infrequently received anything in her life that felt close to what she needed emotionally, so little that had provided her body with the sigh of relief that is true comfort. Pamela was in pain, *in* it and *of* it.

In the many months we had spent getting to know Pamela's childhood experience, we had discovered that "feeling cared for" depended upon feeling known, that one feeling could not exist without the other. Pamela had developed a sense of compassion for her experience of aloneness, of *not-known-ness*. But her compassion for her pain was not available in this moment. There was simply not enough space between her and the emotional tornado that had swallowed her for her to relate with its contents. And so I became that separate place that could be *with* her pain. She was the sadness and I, the larger awareness, the kind container. Together we created a space for her heart to be taken care of.

I asked Pamela if she could bring her awareness into her body, drop into the physical sensations moving inside her. Could she feel what her hands were touching, the air moving across her skin, hear the sounds from the street, experience the beating of her own heart, the vibration of life energy, all the subtle sensations happening inside her at this moment? It was very hard for Pamela to drop out of her mind and into her body, even for a moment to stop telling and re-telling the upsetting story about her husband and her past. She did not want to leave her story behind, loosen her grip on her suffering. For nearly an hour, I continued to encourage her to allow her body to experience its *right now*.

And then something amazing happened: Pamela heard me with a different set of ears, the ears of awareness. As if through a chute in time, Pamela dropped out of the past and into her now. In that present moment, directly experienced by her body, there was no pain, just an experience of "rich aliveness," as she described it. "In my body, I actually feel well at this moment. I am well," she remarked, laughing. The emotions presented as sensation, but without the narrative that went with the sensation, there was just the tightness and a squeezing of sorts. She noticed too that she was a little hungry, and she felt a lot of moving energy, but remarkably, she was free from the rage and suffering that had consumed her. Her body held none of the pain that her mind had been dousing her in for days. "I can love my husband again," she said, spontaneously. From her body's now, Pamela was free to be well.

The body lives in this moment; it is the only place the body can live. It is our mind that travels to and fro between the past and future, never allowing the body to rest in its natural state or time zone. Pamela felt a sense of freedom when she checked out of her mind's pain and into her body's direct experience. She was aware too, that this newfound freedom came with a choice. She could choose to go back and scoop up the hurt from her husband's comment, re-engage, and pull it back into her now. Or, she could stay with what was happening in her body's now and respond to what the current moment was presenting. "Wow, it's like I would have to decide to go back there and pick up that pain, inject myself with it. If I just drop into what's here, I feel a sense of great spaciousness, and even a hint of joy. It's bizarre, where did all that pain that was here just a second ago go?"

Tapping into the body's physical-right-now offers an eject button from the prison of emotional suffering. When we drop down into the experience that the body is living right now, we cannot stay attached to our story about the past or future.

Consider the idea that, as a child, you were bitten by a dog. The body has a cellular memory, and consequently, your adult body may still experience a physical sensation when it sees a dog, perhaps some form of constriction or tightening. And yet, the sensation that arises in you as an adult, if lived directly as a sensation, contains none of the story that goes with the biting, none of the emotional or mental associations, the *why* you were exposed to the dog, *how* your caretakers responded, *what* the biting did to you psychologically, and so on. The story that the mind constructed out of that earlier event is absent and you are left with the stripped-down, direct sensation. As it is, the sensation occurring in the present, even when triggered by something painful or frightening in the past, is almost always bearable, and sometimes even interesting when offered our curiosity.

AFRAID OF THE NOW?

Given that the body is naturally free from the contents of emotional suffering, why do we intentionally introduce it, inflict ourselves with pain, imprison ourselves in torment? Why do we insist on burdening our body's present with the past, our sensations with suffering? Creating space between our selves and our thoughts and feelings creates well-being, and yet we cling to our painful thoughts and feelings, forever contaminating our natural state of well-being. If well-being is so good and so readily available, why do we resist it? The answer is that we are afraid, and confused.

We are afraid of what will happen to us if we drop into the body's now and into the simple well-being that is already here, waiting for us to join it. In truth, it is not our aware, true self that is afraid, but rather, our mind that fears this state of well-being. The mind is a primitive species. It does not have our best interests in *mind*, although it believes it does. Unfortunately, the mind is not as smart as it thinks. The mind has one objective: survival. Because the mind believes that *we* and *it* are one, the mind fights for us by fighting for itself.

We are confused. We believe ourselves to be mind, but, in truth, we are much larger than mind. Our mind is a wonderful tool, but only a tool to be used by our larger identity. Our confusion stems from our not yet having realized our true identity. As long as we believe ourselves to be mind, we will continue to make bad choices, to choose un-well-being over well-being. The real work is in uncovering our true identity, but for now ... we turn our attention to fear.

What is the mind so afraid of in the now? If we were to start living in our body's now, could our lives ever get better? Do we not have to consider what we lived in the past, in order to change what didn't work before? Don't we need to be reminded of our thoughts and emotions in order to improve the present and help guide our future? Surely it would be irresponsible and unwise to live the now that is just here! What if we stray into a kind of Never Never Land of denial? Isn't living just now really an excuse for avoiding our real problems and reality in general? Isn't being a responsible person in society about considering the past and future?

On a more primal level, the mind fears that it will die in the now. To let go of our primary identification with thoughts and feelings would be to agree to our own extinction. Without our thoughts and feelings, who would be left to experience our life? And furthermore, what life would be left to be experienced? The mind believes that we are not safe if we do not continually remind ourselves of who we are, what we believe, what has happened to us. Our stories solidify our identity, maintain our *I*, shore up the borders inside which we are safe from the world. We must be reminded of where we begin and end, keep our defenses from the past up to date. To live in the now would be to live undefended, open, and exposed. If we don't remind ourselves of ourselves, will we not disappear? Unseen and undocumented, is there still an *I*? The fears abound.

To fully enter now would mean that we would have to let go of all the wonderful dilemmas, conundrums, challenges, and dramas that entertain us, keep us busy, and make life the event that it is. To do so would be to give up the very substance of our lives, the material that is *us*. As a friend asked, "What kind of life could there be without the drama of mind, all my stories? What would I do all day? It would all be too still and dull for my liking. No pizzazz, just dead space. My life story is the clay out of which I sculpt . . . life. There would be nothing without it!" Another friend commented, "If I were to just live in the present, all the stuff would vanish, and me with it. It would all just be one big vacuum. Too much to lose."

The mind's fear that it will die in the now is, in part, valid.

Our emotions and thoughts provide us with a sense of solidness, something we can hold onto, a place where we exist in some kind of tangible way. Without thoughts and feelings to cling to, we are just the sensations arising right now, coming and going endlessly.

formed self. In the moment of noticing, the microscope lens pulls back and we expand our perspective to include this new object, this new *somebody,* in an even larger awareness, and the muscle of awareness grows stronger. The process of continually dissolving the forming self is the practice of becoming presence, which character-izes well-being.

Becoming awareness is a life-long practice, not a one-time event. We must keep practicing, reminding ourselves to ask: *Who is this* I *who is looking at the world?* The practice of becoming pres-ence requires that we continue to put our *selves* on the microscope slide, that there be no eye that looks through the lens which is not observed by a larger eye. Through the process, we expand into larger, more spacious versions of ourselves, able to hold ever more in our awareness.

PRACTICE

More than a Mind-Tamer

My first thought of the day is usually about iced coffee. For me, iced coffee is one of the great pleasures of life. When I first began my meditation practice many moons ago, I was doing a concentration practice. I woke up, took my seat on the pillow, and, for lack of a better word, *forced* myself to keep my attention on the breath for however long I had decided I would practice. Amazing how many varieties of iced-coffee thoughts the mind can create! Over and over they would come in, vying for my attention. "A latte? Cinnamon ... nutmeg?" But then I would remember to shift my attention back to the breath. As soon as I was finished with my meditation, I would make my iced coffee and that was the end of it. As time went on, I found it unsatisfying to simply substitute one object of focus for an-other—to use the breath, in a sense, to trump the iced coffee. I was encouraged to see that I could control my attention to some degree, but there had to be more to meditation than strength training. I could not get to the sense of presence simply by establishing control over my mind. I needed to spend more time *with* and *in* whatever force was underneath the thoughts of ice coffee, the force that was directing my attention back to the breath.

More Than a Witness

The next stop on my practice path was mindfulness meditation. I became a witness to my own thoughts, and my own life. I labeled my thoughts and emotions as they arose, observing the machinations of *me*, while keeping my distance at the same time. I became skilled at witnessing. I had found a way to keep from being tossed around in the sea of thoughts, to be less trapped in the turmoil that is my mind, but I was lacking a connection to something larger.

I had left the mind, but without landing anywhere, which was delightful in some ways, but incomplete. When I went out into the world, I found that this mindful and observing witness did not have a voice or heart. I was a set of observing eyes, detached from my experience. From the place of pure witness, not only did I lack access to my heart, but to my joy. I was cut off from the experience of being human. In order to engage in relationship, in life, I had to reenter my ego self, re-identify with my thoughts and feelings, essentially become the mind-centered person I had been before or remain separate—disconnected from the juice of life, interacting from the place of witness. There was no bridge between the witness and the world. Disconnected from the basic well-being that is my embodied core, I was neither thought, nor awareness. I was stuck at a weigh-station in the ether.

Furthermore, as witness I was encased in yet another identity—another version of self. I *was* the transcendent witness, watching my own experience unfold. But I was separate from my experience—and from others—imprisoned by my new non-attached identity. So no matter how relieving it was to be outside what was happening in my life, I would ultimately need to lose my witness identity as well. The witness itself would have to be included in something even larger.

We all need a way to be fully engaged in life and relationship. We are here as human beings after all. It is not enough to disengage from mind (and life), to construct a separate perch from which to hover above our lives, free from the messiness. We need to ground the witness, give her roots in the body. In order for true well-being to emerge, we need to touch into more than just the breath, to utilize the body as more than just a tool for dropping out of mind. Well-being means being able to taste life—be in life—living through our hearts and not our heads. Living through our hearts, we integrate the ground of being human with the sky of seeing.

THE PRACTICE OF PRESENCE/THE PRACTICE OF NOW

The practice of becoming presence is the practice of living a bodily-sensed right now. Presence in the now has a sensation. I have heard it described as weight, life force, fullness, presence, energy, being, strength, electricity, but generally, as some version of *I am home in my body*. Well-being is the practice of moving our awareness, shifting the vantage point from which we are living, from the cage of the mind through the ether of the witness, to the ground of the body. Well-being is the result of dipping into our own aliveness, living the direct experience of right now, not our thoughts about it, just *now* itself. When our body becomes our life's *experiencer*, we have walked through the doorway into true well-being.

Sam showed up in a huff. "Damn trains don't run anymore," he barked, wiping the sweat from his brow. "I stood there waiting for that f'in' train for nearly an hour."

"What was it like to stand on the platform and experience no train?" I asked, carefully.

"It was awful," he said. "I just told you. I was thinking about what you were going to say, and about letting you down and a

million other times in my life when I have been criticized for being late."

"And what was all that like to live?" I asked. My question seemed
to push him from agitated to pissed off.

"It was a nightmare. What are you implying?"

Sam then proceeded to show me where he had spent his last
hour—in the land of thought. He described his imagined reaction
(from me) to his lateness, his lifelong failure with time manage-
ment, the ex-wife who berated him for always being late, arriving
late to his daughter's play in third grade, his mother's humiliating
stories about having to induce his birth because he was so late, the
idiotic mayor who couldn't get the city under control, how he wanted to move to the country but couldn't make that happen either .
. . and the list went on. There was no question; Sam had been in a
trance for the last hour of his life.

"So what am I supposed to do in this case?" he said. "In the case
where right now is clearly going to affect my future, where I am
going to miss my session and still pay for it, because of my now? I
don't get it. I mean unless we all want to walk around like frontal
lobe lobotomy patients . . . the now, by nature, is hitched to the
future. It's all very nice to say that now can exist on its own, but it's
just delusion to imagine you can live the now without the future in
mind!"

Again I asked Sam what it was like to be on that platform without any train in sight, to experience that no-train situation.

Pissed off was now transforming into furious. "A nightmare," he
barked. "Why do you keep asking me what it was like?"

Sam's mind had generated a bevy of thoughts about the experience he was having. Sam had lived the *thoughts* rather than what
was actually happening. The thoughts were the nightmare. "I keep
asking because I have not heard what the experience itself was like.
So far, I have only learned what you think about what happened,"
I offered, not knowing if this would be helpful. He sat quietly for

the first time in the session. After a few beats, I entered the silence, asking Sam if he could imagine stepping *inside* that time on the platform, directly experiencing the energy and sensation inside him as he lived it, the swirling, the prickliness, the heat, and staying with all that without hitching any of it to a story and what it meant about him and his life.

We can, at any moment, no matter what the moment holds, drop out of our thoughts and directly feel what it is like to be where we are. Entering the body's experience is the way to create *presentness*, to find our way back home inside ourselves. Suddenly we are here again, or here for the first time, deposited into the present moment. Our real experience is not *about* the now, it *is* the now.

Sam broke out laughing, usually a good indication that a shift has occurred. "Oh, I get it," he said. "So then everything becomes livable, something to check out, not something I have to get away from! If I don't dive into my stories about me and lateness and everything that has happened to me in the last fifty-three years, well then, I suppose standing on that hot platform could almost become an interesting event! If I were to actually ride what was happening without labeling it anything, it might be kind of a wild trip. I think I get it: it's not my ideas about the discomfort, it's the discomfort itself."

WELL-BEING IS NATURAL

Well-being is the result of holding our own presence in whatever experience is arising. Within this presence, there is no reason to ever have to leave the container of now.

The body's natural state is well-being. Underneath the mind's agitation is a body that can be still, can be in the now, can *be*. Unlike the mind, the body is not in a state of relentless craving, does not require a problem to solve or a task to accomplish. When we bring our awareness into our body, we are training ourselves to come home to our natural state of well-being. We stay home in the body as we ride out the mind's flailings, not attempting to change, calm, or even re-direct the mind. We allow the mind to be the mind, allowing its material to pass through the well-being of the body, into and out of the now.

There is a common misunderstanding that being present means only living what's happening in the body and checking out of the rest of life. As my friend Belinda remarked, "I guess I am not a candidate for being present or what you call well-being since I need to make plans, and if nothing else, make dinner. I can't just walk around feeling my feet against the pavement, although that sounds lovely. I have things I need to think about that are in the future." While it is true that well-being requires a physical presence in the now, this presence includes thoughts about what we need to do for our future as well as what happened in the past. Much of what we do is in some way planning for our future. We make reservations, write shopping lists, interview for jobs; we are constantly involved in activities that relate to our future. Our present includes thinking about our future. However, we can make plans and attend to those future-related tasks without ever leaving our now—staying aware and awake in the direct experience of what we are doing regardless of what or when it is about.

We can and should make use of the wonderful tool that is the mind. We can and should make plans for our future and do all the things that we do in life, but we need not get confused that the mind making the plans, and doing the doing, is who we are. We are the larger presence within which the thoughts about tonight's dinner plans appear. We use our mind to attend to the future while staying rooted and identified with the awareness that sits under what we are doing right now.

STRENGTH TRAINING

The practice of now takes strength. Lisa was on her way home from work, feeling the usual rumblings of her mind's agitation. She no longer had the focus of work to contain her mind's need for entertainment and distraction. She was heading into the Miracle Mile, a stretch of shopping boutiques that lined the town where she lived. This was a dangerous spot for her, a place where her mind sniffed a potential escape route from its primal agitation. She was feeling the undefined, ill-at-ease feeling she always felt at this time of the day. As she put it, "Lost, searching, and without purpose is my 5 P.M. now." In an effort to fill the craving for something unknowable, she was often compelled to shop, aimlessly looking for something that would make her feel better, more complete, less agitated. Lisa didn't need anything new—at least nothing that she could purchase—but still, she felt the longing.

Almost every day after disappearing into the vortex of shopping in the Miracle Mile, Lisa would return home and eventually wake up with new things that she didn't need, the buzz of shopping quickly wearing off—along with the anesthesia it had offered. Lisa enjoyed shopping so the act of it was not unpleasant, but each day she felt more and more sad for the person who was wandering around looking for something unknown, trying unsuccessfully to create a sense of ease or comfort. Her mind, in its natural state of agitation, kept telling her that her *now* was incomplete, not a place she could settle into—not a place she could be.

Could Lisa stay rooted and aware in her 5 P.M. *now*? Could she bear to experience the thoughts, feelings, and physical sensations which drove her to shop, but—and this was the catch—without attending to their demands? Could she live through her mind's need to get out of the moment, without trying to get out of it? Could she meet the agitation, without doing anything about it? I reminded Lisa that she had expressed feeling "sad" for the person wandering around looking for something unknowable, and I asked her to consider *who* it was that felt this sadness for her.

The following day, as she passed the Miracle Mile with these questions in mind, courage in her heart, and fierce determination to meet her emptiness without filling it, Lisa stopped her bike and sat still. She committed to staying still. Her intention was to physically experience the craving to shop, to actually feel the agitation that compelled her to want to escape from her *now*. The first thing Lisa noticed was a severe tightening in her chest. Along with it, a kind of blankness or "deadness descending." Lisa noticed thoughts telling her that she was crazy for standing there, that this exercise was a waste of time and would never help her. She experienced a jitteriness that came with not moving and tidal waves of energy rising and passing within her. On top of all that, a peculiar kind of nausea descended. Lisa noticed all this just sitting still on her bike.

"Several times, I felt myself start to go under, to give in, to just start shopping and buy everything, the whole damn store. I thought, *screw this experiment, and you; I am not up to it, maybe in another lifetime—another stronger incarnation*. I thought I could just quit therapy and then I would never even have to tell you all this. I was so aching for that comforting little cowbell sound that rings when you open the door to the shop on Hines Street. But I caught myself, I heard your voice . . . to feel *that*, as a sensation, whatever *that* was—to make *that* a destination. I heard you tell me to just *stay* with it, that you knew (even if I didn't) that I could bear whatever *that* was there. I told myself that whatever happened I was not going to move. Some part of me was *not* my thoughts, was bigger than my thoughts, and *that* part was going to keep my feet planted. I remembered your words, that all I had to do was keep breathing and stay still, and that it would pass—and it did. But man, that was really hard."

Lisa's practice had lasted twenty minutes, after which time the tsunami inside her subsided. She had lived the actual agitation, directly—and survived it. Lisa had experienced the place that she feared was emptiness; by walking into it, she had turned emptiness into a place of substance—a destination rich with sensorial material. What had seemed like emptiness was in fact, a whole universe of feeling.

When the craving calmed, Lisa felt better than she had in months. Unlike when she wandered aimlessly in the shops, or even when she found something lovely to buy, she did not feel sad or empty after this experience. In fact, she felt just the opposite, as she put it, "really full." Lisa had stayed present with what was happening inside her, living it as it unfolded. She had weathered her experience from inside it, ridden out her mind's agitation as a cowboy rides out a bucking bronco. In those twenty minutes, she had built her awareness muscle and experienced her larger self; the next ride would be a tiny bit easier. Lisa came home without any pretty new things but with a deep sense of her own vastness—and strength. She felt well, and whole.

The more we practice staying with what is arising without reacting to it, the better we get at it. As we do this practice, we build a distinct kind of confidence: a warrior's confidence. We come to trust, through our own effort, that we can tolerate anything and everything that arises, can weather any storm without having to flee the scene, check out on what's here. Nothing is so frightening as to be able to force us out of the now. Through this practice, we develop a fierce internal confidence. As *now* warriors, our strength is grounded in fearlessness.

A POT OF COURAGE

In making the choice to be well, we are deciding to change, to enter a process that is new and, most likely, outside of our comfort zone. Often in creating change we must do away with what is familiar. While our former system may not have worked well, it was known, and there is a strong power and comfort in the known. The choice to change requires a huge pot of courage, the courage to let go of what we know and head in a direction that is dark or barely lit, to enter a place where we don't know the way.

So too, the choice to be well requires the courage to stop—stop doing, stop searching, stop feeding the belief that there is something, somewhere, that will make us whole. Well-being asks that we stop and be still. More often than not, it is the stopping and not the doing that demands the fiercest courage of all.

How and where do we find courage? Sometimes we derive it from a need to alleviate the suffering of un-well-being. At other times we are made brave by a taste of well-being, and the ensuing desire for a whole meal. Sometimes we find the courage—from a source that is unknowable, perhaps well-being itself—to undock our boat from the side of the river and head into unknown waters. Nonetheless, courage must be in the boat with us as we head toward and into change. From where we are, we cannot know exactly what well-being will be like, but we can—and should—honor the courage that the journey of change demands.

THE ADDICTED MONKEY

A lovely, kind, spiritually developed woman in her mid-forties, Nina was, in many ways, well. She was in a healthy marriage, adored her children, was deeply fulfilled and nourished by her work as a social worker, and was connected with her body through a regular yoga practice. However, there was one relationship in her life that Nina was not managing well or, as she phrased it, "Where I am not in control of my own choices." The troublesome relationship was between her and wine, or rather, between her and her thoughts about wine. While she did not drink to excess in terms of quantity, she was an addict in that when the wine thoughts appeared, she felt at their mercy and driven by their demands—her thoughts were the boss. The thoughts usually began dropping in around noon, a light drizzle at first, gradually building to a flood as the day went on. *You could have a glass with lunch,* the thoughts would whisper in her ear. Nina could usually, fairly easily, remind herself that a glass of wine with lunch would make her tired, upset her stomach, monopolize her attention, and effectively ruin the rest of her day. But the thoughts continued, gaining in frequency and volume, conspiring for her attention. As they escalated, her thoughts pulled her further and further away from her present moment, kidnapping her into an imagined future.

When the time came to finally tilt her glass, the experience was not even interesting or particularly pleasurable. "Wine doesn't even relax me or put me in a good mood like it used to," she told me. It had been a long time since the wine itself had offered Nina the enjoyment or relief that the thoughts still promised. As she put it, "My love affair with wine has been over for a long time, but for some reason I continue to spend all my time with *him*, as if he still does something for me. My whole life is being lost to arranging when and how I will get to this future glass of wine, to the future period. And the whole thing I am oriented toward, planning for, thinking about, spending my time with, really, is not even good. I don't drink more than a glass because I barely even like it anymore. It all sounds ridiculous when I say it out loud." The problem for Nina was not with wine, but with her own attention—and *who* was in charge of it.

Nina had tried many different therapies and meditative practices to gain control of or at least build a better relationship with her drinking thoughts. She had learned to observe her thoughts when they appeared. She came to understand them as random firings by a system whose nature was to fire simply out of habit and without purpose. She had practiced logging her drinking thoughts in a journal, keeping track of what she was feeling and who she was with when the thoughts appeared. While all of these practices were helpful, after a period of time she found that she could no longer retain her seat as witness to her thoughts, and ended up surrendering to their demands, and thereby relinquishing the freedom that her awareness had permitted. Sooner or later, her thoughts became too convincing—too seductive to resist, and without awareness, she had united with them yet again.

Nina had practiced talking back to her addictive thoughts, discovering that the grown-up in her could respond to and overrule her childish and irrational thoughts. She became skilled at illuminating their faulty reasoning. "I remind myself that wine just makes me tired and is not in fact a solution to any pain that I am experiencing." While her work had helped to create a bit of separation between her and her thoughts, nonetheless, her thoughts continued to hold the upper hand. She spent the day responding to them, reminding them of their speciousness, relentlessly fending off their demands for her *now*.

Nina had worked on a behavioral level too, learning to change her response to her thoughts by replacing her negative thoughts with positive ones. Each time she heard a drinking thought, she deliberately generated and executed a thought about taking a walk or calling a friend, replacing each incorrect or misinformed thought with one that she considered wise and helpful. Calling a friend would bring her the company that the thought was incorrectly telling her existed in the wine. Taking a walk would bring her the physical sensation of well-being that the thought was mistakenly telling her existed in the alcohol. She took a lot more walks and called a lot more friends but still her *now* was controlled by her interaction with her thoughts. Her response to her thoughts had changed, but the problem with her *now* remained.

Nina had spent years exploring her early childhood, examining her relationships with her parents, and the sense of emptiness and fragility that those relationships had created in her. She understood that her mother's inability to comfort her had left her with a sense of un-soothe-able anxiety—the anxiety that the wine had initially dulled. She was aware that her father's emotional distance had left her always trying to land somewhere but never finding *there*. She was aware that the relationship with her father had created a primal void in her, as she had tried desperately, and futilely, to connect with him on a level that felt real. Nina had compassion for the anxiety that had initially triggered her desire for wine. She understood its roots and even agreed with its reasoning.

Furthermore, Nina had learned to examine the feelings that were present at the moment her wine thoughts appeared. She could ask herself, *What feeling in this moment needs to be sedated? What am I trying to get away from inside?* More often than not she could figure out precisely what was bothering her, the experience that was not welcome, and thus needing anesthesia. And yet, all her understanding, all her good work, did not stop the thoughts from coming, stalking her, and rarely interrupted the behavior that followed. She understood in great detail who, what, where, when, and why she did not want to feel, and that knowledge kept her company all the way to the wine cabinet.

Nina had a lot of tools, skills, and knowledge. What she didn't have was her freedom. It wasn't important anymore why she was having these thoughts or even what the thoughts were about. We could spend the next ten years coming up with valid reasons and stories for each of the thoughts that randomly fired in her mind. Nothing was changing. No new experience was arriving. Despite all of her rigorous and intelligent attempts to defeat her thoughts, her thoughts were defeating her.

Living with this constant distraction was exhausting, and Nina was growing weary and hopeless. She was missing her life, trapped inside a hamster's habit-trail of something that didn't even interest her. As she put it, "Why can't I just have the damn glass of wine at six P.M.? I would be fine with that. I can decide what sort and where I will have it at 5:59. Trust me, I am not flying in bottles from France that would need my attention at noon! I would like to actually live the wine when I am living the wine, and live the rest of my life when I am living the rest of my life."

The moments of Nina's day were not places to land but rather part of a trajectory course to a future destination, "a whooshing missile" that made it impossible for her to stop and dip into any of the present moments along the way. Until the ride to the future was completed, culminating in "a glass of bad chardonnay," Nina was shut out from her *now*, trapped always on a path to *then*.

Nina needed a radical new approach. Since all attempts to remove or change her thoughts had failed; rather than design another approach to make *what was* into something different, she needed a way to make *what was* actually work for her—a path that would allow Nina's wine thoughts to be included in her now—without commanding her attention. We needed to return Nina to the space that existed around her thoughts, the field in which her thoughts fired. Rather than obstacles to *present-ness*, Nina's thoughts needed to become actual invitations into her *now*.

I suggested to Nina that the contents or time frame of her thoughts, whether about a past or future event, did not have to dictate where her attention traveled or resided. Her thoughts were about something that would happen in the future, specifically 6 P.M., when she would have her first glass of wine. The contents of her thoughts had a local time zone: the future. But the thoughts themselves, the synapses in her brain, were actually firing right now; the sensations they were triggering were now. It was all happening now, nowhere else—no other time. Paying attention to the experience of her thoughts—not what they were talking about—then would require staying in the moment where it was all happening.

We can experience a thought as an event or sensation that is occurring right now, which is precisely what it is—something completely out of our control, and not something we need to do anything about.

I asked Nina if she could imagine residing in the present moment with a kind of expectant curiosity, as if she had a camera pointed at an empty landscape, the landscape of her own mind. Could she await her own thoughts with a sense of wonder, as you might await a morning bird's call or the appearance of a deer? Could she sense the physical reaction, the sensation of wanting, that occurred when a thought appeared in her internal landscape? Likewise, could she experience her *now* with the thoughts of wine inside it, observing, but not changing or responding to what was there?

This approach immediately resonated with Nina. "It is almost as if the thought becomes just another animal passing through the space that is me, my body. If I can include the thought, but without its contents, then I can stay in the present—maybe even attend to what else is there besides the thought. I don't have to fixate on just that particular animal; it's like I can pull the lens of my camera back and see the whole landscape," she exclaimed.

WATCHING CLOUDS

We need permission to stop doing anything with our thoughts, to just allow them to wander in and out. By allowing our thoughts to simply happen, without much ado (like any other naturally occurring phenomenon) we strip them of their power. Without the pressure to travel to the time zone that our thoughts are pointing to, we can relax and stay in the present as our thoughts come and go in and out of our field of awareness. Suddenly, there is a wider space in which we can reside, and we are freed up to see—and live—a much larger experience.

A presence exists that is not made of thought—a presence that does not need an object of focus—the presence of simply being. When we are no longer tethered to the contents of our thoughts, feelings, and sensations, but can watch them wander in and out of our field of vision, we are free to settle back into this larger presence of being, to live from and become this larger awareness—our true self.

There is no need to ever leave the moment, to leave presence. Whatever arises in our internal landscape is a part of the present moment, and thus something else to be included in the landscape that is *now*, to be noticed and experienced—or not. The choice is ours. Our thoughts, feelings, and sensations are not intruders, there to drag us out and away from the present moment. What is important is that our view remains wide—that *we* remain wide— living from the larger presence through which it is all moving.

With everything included, there can be no obstacle to our presence in the now.

With our lens wide and unconditionally inclusive, reality takes on a different direction. The experience of life shifts from a horizontal reality in which we are traveling backward and forward along a finite time line—past, future, and eventually death—never dropping in to visit this now, to a vertical reality in which all experiences are occurring in and through a single point—the point of now. We ride only the point of now with the past and future ceasing to exist as separate, individual destinations. No longer something finite that moves from a beginning to an end, life becomes an ongoing experience of present moments with each moment containing its own *vertical* infinity.

9   MELTING INTO *NOW*

What happens when the *I* who is having or noticing the experience melts into the experience itself? What remains when the separation between *what* is being experienced and *who* is experiencing it disintegrates? If the answers to these questions remain unclear, that is okay—it is in fact, a good thing. These are not riddles to solve. Just inviting the questions into the body, allowing yourself to marinate in them without trying to answer them, is an exercise that generates its own evolution. The marination itself is part of the practice.

LOOSENING OUR GRIP

Our *I* is a point of reference. We look out at the world from *I*; everything we experience is filtered through it and by it. Venturing from our *I* point of reference, we hunt down our experience, grab it, constrict around it—possess it. It is as if we are heat-seeking missiles sent into the field of consciousness to capture and solidify anything that is moving, namely, thoughts, feelings, and sensations. On the other hand, when we relax and allow everything to be included inside the now, we loosen the grip on our experience and, with it, our point of reference. The *I* that was there previously dissolves as a fixed and identifiable entity; we are set free. Aware of what is arising, we remain rooted in presence, but not from any particular place. Released from the confines of a vantage point, *as* this new place-less awareness, we are liberated to enter experience directly. We then slip from the cage of the finite into the unbounded and limitless—the *beyond*.

I asked Caroline, a photographer, if she could experience *how she was in that moment, from the inside*, clarifying that it was an invitation not a question. She responded: "I am really upset because . . ." and began to tell me a story about something that had happened with one of her employees. Early in the story I stopped her and asked again if she could experience how she was from the inside. She paused, "I'm pissed off and really disappointed." I too paused, and then asked the same question a third time. Caroline looked perplexed, but when I did not respond, she readjusted herself and took on a different expression. This time she seemed to be checking in with her body, looking inside for a different kind of answer. After a few moments, she reported that she noticed a strong pain in her chest and that her ankles felt jumpy and twitchy. We were headed in the right direction; the answer was about her body. Still, I wanted her to go further. I asked her if she could lose the *noticer* too, and just experience what she was experiencing—feel the pain and twitchiness directly without reporting the sensations. I asked her to imagine an image clicking into its frame, so that only one experience existed and no longer an experience and an *experiencer.*

Caroline relaxed with this invitation. When she spoke again, she said this: "It was as if I was just a part of the experience or maybe I *was* the experience. There was sensation and emotion, but without the story of it. A lot of movement, a lot period, but I was in it. No, not exactly, it was more like I *was* it, not separate from it, describing it, understanding it—just it. I was inside what I was living, or rather, I was what I was living, in the happening. How amazing!"

This is what the place beyond well-being feels like. We enter experience, not as witness—perched above—and not as ego—identified with contents—but as the awareness inside the experience itself, the heat within the flame. With this entry comes a kind of joy that is palpable. We are free from the ego's story *about* our experience and released from the isolation that being separate from our experience creates. The casing around us dissolves and we become part of what we are living.

As blissful as this new freedom is, our habit is to re-form a separate self, remind ourselves of our selves, of who we are, re-trace our outlines. Nonetheless, the invitation to live our experience directly, to *be* our experience, remains. From happiness to well-being to beyond is a path from chasing the *now*, to being *with* the now, to becoming the *now*.

I remember the moment when I first received the instruction to *do nothing* in my meditation practice. Funny enough, this was a huge ah-ha moment in my evolution. I had never been a *do nothing* kind of woman, so this teaching called for a true paradigm shift. With the instruction to stop doing, I suddenly had permission to stop managing what was happening inside me, stop managing *me*. Easier said than done (or not done!). My practice then was to permit whatever was happening in my consciousness to just happen. If I noticed myself trying to manage my meditation and simultaneously trying to stop managing it, I could let that happen too. The part of me that was noticing could just sit back and do nothing. I was free from the doing. Furthermore, I did not need to make my awareness expand or contract; it could just be as it was. In truth, my managing self could not return me to awareness even if it wanted to. Only by letting go of control, stopping the trying, could awareness find its way home—to itself. My only job was to stay there while it all happened, to maintain my seat as presence—without becoming any of the *happenings*.

Not doing allows us to settle back into the larger awareness that is already here before the meditation begins, beneath the thoughts. With the managing *I* out of the way, awareness is free to enter the present experience as the light that illuminates what is seen.

In the space beyond well-being, we no longer need a separate, boundaried self to protect us and keep us safe inside its walls. Rather than a self that protects its existence by remaining separate, beyond well-being is a place where experience arises and we, as the awareness inside it, are safe to join in that arising.

Over the years, I have noticed one longing that virtually all human beings share. While some feel it more explicitly than others, I have yet to meet anyone who does not crave returning to an experience of oneness, a place where we are not separate—not alone. As embodied human beings, we long to be one and not two, to be folded into our larger source. We seek relief from the suffering that our boundaried, and thus isolated, nature creates. In describing this longing for unity, we use words like *come home, return, reconnect*. Our language suggests that we will be absorbed or welcomed back into a previously-known state of being when we were one and not two, not separate from our experience—or each other.

Perhaps the craving is for a return to our mother's womb, or perhaps to the life source in which we existed before being birthed into a separated body. But wherever the memory of our oneness stems from, we are in a constant search to satisfy it. We find relief from our separateness—temporarily—inside a hug from our child; in the falling into love; in the oneness of sexuality; during flow states of deep mental or physical involvement or supreme attention; and, in a less evolved forms, through addictions. But our aloneness soon returns, and we must again set out to find the unity that we crave.

Remarkably, as the separate self dissolves, so too does our fundamental isolation. In the melting of the boundaried self, we find relief from our primal aloneness; we uncover the lasting peace of returning to a bodily-known state of wholeness. Moving beyond well-being is a process of coming home to the presence that is already here—always here—of re-joining who we are, not temporarily, but eternally.

10   LIVING AS AWARENESS

We have traveled a journey together over these pages. When we started we were chasing happiness, trying to organize and control our internal and external experience in order to create a life and an identity that was pleasurable. It was an unreliable and unsuccessful attempt to make ourselves okay, by making life go *our way*. In the process, we were making ourselves not okay, mistreating our own experience, conducting an unkind relationship with our selves.

We then considered a different destination, a different goal for our lives—well-being, rather than happiness. As we've noted in chapter after chapter, well-being is a state that is not dependent upon the contents of our life going our way or any other way. We can be well even when our life situation is not pleasing, when our experience is not happy. While well-being does not rely on any particular situation, it does require that we learn a new way of being in relationship with our experience. This new relationship demands an evolution in both our awareness and our identity. Indeed, our sense of who we are—*who* is experiencing our life—shifts in the process of discovering, and uncovering, well-being.

At the beginning of this journey, we are unaware, asleep in the cockpit. We are whatever bird is moving through the sky of our consciousness. Our awareness then awakens and we begin to see our experience, watch it pass through our consciousness, be *with* it—not *of* it. Awareness then grows wider and stronger, big enough to see not only our experience but also the space around—the space in which our experience is happening—the birds *and* the sky. Finally, awareness expands so wide as to be able to include itself; awareness becomes aware of awareness, with nothing outside of its field of knowing.

If we were to track the shift in identity that takes place along this journey, we could say that we start as **a defined separate self**, fully identified with our opinions, feelings, beliefs, sensations, and all the rest. We are our accomplishments, titles, and possessions. There is only ego self. We then evolve into **the compassionate witness**, the self that can watch our experience, be in kind relationship with our thoughts, feelings, and sensations, but with some separateness from the contents of what we live. From there, we become aligned with **the spaciousness** that surrounds our experience, without any fixed location, the silence into which the notes enter. Finally, anchoring this spaciousness into the body, we experience ourselves **as awareness itself**, spaciousness rooted in the ground of being. We are presence, the energy that ignites experience, the awareness that is everywhere and in everything, but identified and identifiable nowhere.

While this is one path of a self's progression, the dissolution or—evolution—of our identity follows no defined route. For some, the separate self can explode in an instant, without any traces of having been encased, and without any of the steps mentioned. For others, identity shifts occur in small increments, with many glimpses of clarity occurring over long periods of time. The process can unfold in an infinite array of designs and patterns. There is no right progression on the path to becoming who we are.

While awareness is always here, a constant, the quality of awareness is ever changing. In those times when I am very busy in my daily life, awareness is there in the background in a kind of light and airy way. I am that light *being* behind all the tasks, responsibilities, and demands. At other times, awareness makes itself known in a deep and resonant presence, a bass hum under everything, with all of life echoing within it. And sometimes awareness is a dancing aliveness, an effervescent light that illuminates all experience. As my practice continues, I am less concerned by how awareness is presenting itself or how close or distant it feels. Regardless of how much of my ego self is currently being employed in the world,

I know that awareness is still here underneath the movement of mind, always available for me to come home to. While certain presentations of awareness (the deep and resonant sort) are more enjoyable to live, awareness—like everything else—is in constant flux. The style in which it is momentarily manifesting is unrelated to its presence or, for that matter, to our being made of that presence.

As we practice in daily life, we build an awareness that can be aware of the location of our own attention. One eye remains open inside—awake to where we are bringing our focus. As I busily move through my job and family responsibilities, my mind is needed for the tasks of life. And yet, awareness can still be present and aware of where my local attention is residing. If my attention is needed in a task, I can be fully in the task while also aware that I am there. When a specific emotion calls for my attention, my company, I can attend to that emotion while remaining aware that I am there. Even when I am caught inside a thought, awareness can be aware that I am caught. In this way, the location of our attention can be fluid while a larger awareness that includes even our attention becomes continuous. We can stay rooted in the stillness of this larger awareness regardless of where we are momentarily choosing to focus it. In the same way that Rumi in the poem, "The Guest House" (see Introduction), invites us to welcome all of our emotions as *houseguests* into our being, so too, our attention can be welcome wherever it is residing, without our having to give up anything.

We are creatures of habit. Our strongest habit is to return to the familiar, the known. As we uncover well-being and awareness practice, our habit is to shrink from the larger awareness and crawl back into our ego concerns, return to the mind's known environs. But well-being practice also includes an awareness of our habits, and a choice to refrain from indulging them; awareness allows us to welcome our fear of expansion and change, to stay present with the fear, but without changing our course. Furthermore, when we notice our desire to shrink, something wonderful is already happening: we are expanding, growing our awareness, and shedding more of our separate *I*-casing. We are breaking free into our larger self. This expanding, shrinking, and re-expanding process is unending, facilitated and buoyed by self-kindness. Little by little, we evolve—and dissolve—into something blissful, infinite, and reliably well.

11 POINTERS

Over time, I have found it helpful to keep close a small journal of phrases that remind me of the path from happiness to well-being and beyond. Our spiritual practice must continue throughout the day and not just for the time we spend meditating. In order to keep expanding into well-being and indeed the bliss that sits beyond it, our practice must be a moment-to-moment occurrence. Sometimes a single word or phrase, when it's the right one, can wake us up—in an instant—return us to awareness, and to our true self. Ironically, something that is generally a product of our mind, namely, words, also holds the power to catapult us out of mind. Words, well chosen, can invite us into the experience of just being, as if they were the language of the true self. Luckily, such words do not ask our mind's permission to depart from it as an identity, but rather, drop us directly into awareness, which recognizes itself as our home and who we are, even when we need to be reminded. What follows is a list of short phrases that serve as my personal wake-up calls, the little sayings that *un-stick* me from my small, ego mind self— explode my *I*, and send me into the larger experience of awareness, of *now-ness*. I am grateful to these words for their capacity to turn my inner dial from noise to silence—to provide me entry into my own well-being.

POINTERS

Un-sticking: *Dropping out of mind*
Let life happen
Change nothing

INVITING A MONKEY TO TEA

Loosen your grip
Let be
Allow
Relax around the thoughts
Stop trying to be a better version of yourself
Stop trying
Stop searching
Just stop
It's already here
Rest your mind
Drop the backpack of mind
Take a break from mind
Kindness for this mind
Kindness for this creature
Soften your mind
Unhook from mind
Give up control
Surrender
Be nobody
Welcome this now
Soft focus your mind
Relax in the chaos
Nothing to accomplish
Make no effort

Being Spacious
Find the silence between the noise
Find the stillness
Life is happening, no one is living it
Observe don't change
Feel the space between and around the thoughts
You are not the thinking mind
You are the space within which all phenomena appears

Let go of the bird and be the sky
Be spacious
Be space
Rest in the space
Find the all that surrounds the small
Widen your lens
Listen for God
Await God

Grounding/Coming home into the body

Feel now
Feel the body
Experience what you are experiencing
Receive what's here
Feel your presence
Feel now
Feel the presence of space
Feel the inside of your body
Feel stillness
Feel being alive
Feel being
Invite what's here
Come into here
Find your attention
Be with you
Drop into your heart
Drop into yourself
Join yourself
Return to source
Feel what's underneath the thoughts
Feel the source of all thought
Follow the breath home
Stay here

Everything you need is here
Drop into God
God dwells in you as you

Entering Now
What's here?
Receive what's here
Open to what is here
Always now
Feel now
Drop into now
Surrender into now
Enter now
Join this moment
Synch your attention with now

Invitations into presence—**questions to marinate in (not answer)**
Who is hearing these thoughts?
Who is receiving these sounds?
Who is feeling these sensations?
Who is here?
What is alive?
Who is aware?
Who am I?
Who is underneath the thoughts?
What is still?
Who knows that I am alive?
What if this moment were all there is?
What thought will I have next?
 What does here feel like?
What if this moment were my last?

I offer these phrases for you to sample. Take each one for a test run, for a day, a week, a month, whatever works. Notice the effect that the words have on your body, your awareness, and your being. At the same time, I encourage you to come up with your own words. What melts my separateness might not even heat the pebbles beneath your ego's feet. Sometimes simply substituting an *into* for an *in* can birth an entire paradigm shift. Language makes a difference. The fact that what works for each of us differs so widely is a wonderful testament to our individuality, and the uniqueness that exists within our embodied borders.

Our distinctions are real. At the same time, we are not separate. That which makes us who we are as individuals, our likes and dislikes, are characteristics of our *human-ness*. Like everything else, our *human-ness* is included in the larger awareness that is our being-ness, and our true identity. Through the eyes of our larger self, we can notice, include and celebrate our unique qualities, our individual monkeys, but without singularly identifying with them or using them to confine us into separate *I s*. We remain identified with the larger awareness while noticing (and celebrating) our unique human designs.

I carry a photograph of a wide blue sky with a small bird flying through it and a desert floor below. This image instantly relocates *me* from riding whatever is moving through my consciousness into the larger sky of awareness, while simultaneously grounding me in this earth-bound body. But I invite you to discover your own words, questions, sounds, smells, sights, and whatever else helps release you from the limitations of the separate and small mind, the happy or sad self. I encourage you to find the tools that lead and deliver you into the awareness that is already here, waiting for you to come home—to yourself

As we travel on this path, we must remember that awareness (and thus well-being) is always here, never further than this patch of dirt on which we are standing. Our path is made up of infinite *right heres*, each footstep a place to inhabit—to be. The journey into well-being and beyond is a journey into here. If I can offer you anything through this work, may it be an invitation to stop searching, welcome the monkey, and come home to the presence that awaits— inside of you and inside of now.

RESOURCES

AUTHORS/WEBSITES

Advaita Vedanta information (*www.realization.org*)
Eckhart Tolle (*www.eckharttolle.com*)
Gangaji (*www.gangaji.com*)
Katherine Ingram (*www.dharmadialogues.com*)
Loch Kelly (*www.lochkelly.org*)
Mooji (*www.mooji.org*)
Nancy Colier (*www.nancysc.com*)
Osho (*www.osho.com*)
Papaji (*www.avadhuta.com*)
Pema Chödrön (*www.pemachodronfoundation.org*)
Ramana Maharshi (*www.sriramanamaharshi.org*)
Sri Ramakrishna (*www.ramakrishna.org*)
Surya Das (*www.surya.org*)

BOOKS AND CDS

Adyashanti. *The End of Your World*. Sounds True Inc, Boulder, CO, 2008.

Bayda, Ezra. *Being Zen: Bringing Meditation to Life*. Shambhala Publications, Boston, MA, 2002.

Brach, Tara. *Radical Acceptance*. Bantam Dell, New York, NY, 2003.

Chödrön, Pema. *Getting Unstuck* (Audio). Sounds True Inc, Boulder, CO, 2010.

Chödrön, Pema. *Start Where You Are: A Guide to Compassionate Living*. Shambhala Publications, Boston, MA, 1994.

Chögyam, Trungpa. *The Sacred Path of a Warrior.* Shambhala Publications, Boston, MA, 1984.

Gangaji. *The Diamond in Your Pocket.* Sounds True Inc, Boulder, CO, 2007.

Gangaji. *You Are That.* Sounds True, Inc, Boulder, CO, 2007.

Ingram, Catherine. *A Crack In Everything.* Diamond Books, Portland, OR, 2006.

Ingram, Catherine. *Passionate Presence.* Diamond Books, Portland, OR, 2008.

Kidd, Sue Monk. *When the Heart Waits: Spiritual Direction for Life's Sacred Questions.* Harper&Row, San Francisco, CA, 1990.

Kornfield, Jack. *A Path With Heart.* Bantam Books, New York, NY, 1993.

Maharaj, Sri Nisargadatta. *I Am That.* Acorn Press, Durham, NC, 1973.

Maharshi, Ramana. *The Spiritual Teachings of Ramana Maharshi.* Shambhala Publications, Boston, MA, 2004.

Mipham, Rinpoche Sakyong. *Turning the Mind Into an Ally.* Riverhead Books, New York, NY, 2003.

Osho. *Awareness.* St. Martin's Press, New York, NY, 2001.

Red Hawk. *Self Observation.* Hohm Press, Prescott, AZ, 2009.

Salzberg, Sharon. *Lovingkindness: The Revolutionary Art of Happiness.* Shambhala Publications Inc, Boston, MA, 1997.

Shainberg, Diane. *Chasing Elephants.* Asti-Rahman Books, New York NY, 2000.

Shainberg, Nancy. *Getting Out of Your Own Way: Unlocking Your True Performance Potential.* Luminous Press, New York, NY, 2001.

Singer, Michael A. *The Untethered Soul.* New Harbinger Publications Inc. and Noetic Books, Oakland, CA, 2007.

Teasdale, Wayne. *Mystic Heart.* New World Library, Novato, CA, 1999.

The Dalai Lama, and Cutler, Howard. *The Art of Happiness.* Riverhead Books, New York, NY, 1998.

Tolle, Eckhart. *The Power of Now.* New World Library, Novato, CA, 1999.

Welwood, John. *Toward a Psychology of Awakening.* Shambhala Publications, Boston, MA, 2000.

ENDNOTES

1. Wallace, Alan B., Jacobs, Tonya, Saron, Clifford, Blackburn, Elizabeth, Epel, Elissa, Lin, Jue, and Wolkowitz, Owen. "The Shamatha Project: Training Attention and Emotion Regulation through Intensive Meditation." Santa Barbara Institute for Consciousness Studies. 2010.
2. "Cultivating Compassion: Neuro-Scientific and Behaviorial Approaches." Richard J. Davidson, The Center for Compassion and Altruism Research and Education, 2010.
3. Loch Kelly. Natural Wakefulness Center, New York, NY. *www.lochkelly.org*

INDEX

Index